P&A CAMPBELL
STEAMERS

P&A CAMPBELL
STEAMERS

THE
Edwardian
ERA

CHRIS COLLARD

TEMPUS

Frontispiece: *Capt. Peter Campbell on the bridge of* Britannia *at Ilfracombe on 21 July 1910. The story is told of how Peter, swinging the* Britannia *at Bristol late one night, let fly with a torrent of bad language directed at one of the seamen on the foredeck who had fumbled a rope. An elderly lady, standing just below the bridge wing, was horrified at his outburst and said to him, 'Captain, I shall report you to the managing director!' Peter leaned over the bridge and replied, 'Madam. I am the managing director. And I apologize for my language'.*

First published 2006

Tempus Publishing Limited
The Mill, Brimscombe Port,
Stroud, Gloucestershire, GL5 2QG
www.tempus-publishing.com

© Chris Collard, 2006

The right of Chris Collard to be identified as the Author
of this work has been asserted in accordance with the
Copyrights, Designs and Patents Act 1988.

British Library Cataloguing in Publication Data.
A catalogue record for this book is available from the British Library.

ISBN 0 7524 3871 9

Typesetting and origination by Tempus Publishing Limited
Printed in Great Britain

Contents

SOURCES AND ACKNOWLEDGEMENTS

An unpublished manuscript by the late Capt. Daniel Taylor, by courtesy of his sons, the late Alec and the late Archie Taylor.

The surviving records of P&A Campbell Ltd, by courtesy of the Bristol Records Office.

The records of the Ailsa Shipbuilding & Engineering Co. Ltd, Troon, and of John Brown & Co. Ltd, Clydebank, by courtesy of the University of Glasgow Archives.

The records of the Barry Railway Co. Some details of: the Lyn Steamship Co., the Brighton, Worthing & South Coast Steamboat Co., the Sussex Steam Packet Co. Ltd, the Roman Steamship Co. Ltd, the Bristol Channel Express Steamboat Co. Ltd, the Bristol Channel Passenger Service Ltd, the Lady Margaret Steamship Co. Ltd, the Lord Tredegar Steamship Co. Ltd. Correspondence of the Marine Department of the Board of Trade – all courtesy of the Public Record Office, Kew.

Some records of Birnbeck Pier, Weston Super Mare, courtesy of the late Capt. E. J. Wide.

Some records of Barclay Curle & Co. Ltd., courtesy of William Lind.

Custom House Registers for Belfast, Bristol, Cardiff, Leith, London and Shoreham courtesy of HM Customs, King's Beam House, London.

Bristol Museum & Art Gallery.

British Museum Newspaper Library, Colindale, London.

Cardiff Public Libraries.

National Maritime Museum, Greenwich, London.

Newport Museum & Art Gallery.

Registrar General of Shipping & Seamen, Gabalfa, Cardiff.

National Archives of Scotland, (formerly the Scottish Records Office).

Strathclyde Archives, Mitchell Library, Glasgow.

The former Welsh Industrial & Maritime Museum.

Woodspring Museum.

The author also wishes to express his sincere gratitude to the following individuals:

Dr Donald Anderson, Tom Bartlett, Revd Norman Bird, John Brown, Richard Clammer, Nigel Coombes, Dr. David Jenkins, Ken Jenkins, William Lind, Sydney Robinson, Mike Tedstone, Phillip Tolley, Lionel Vaughan, Admeto Verde.

The late Mrs Gordon Fry, (*née* Helen Hunter Campbell – Capt. Peter's daughter Nellie).

The late Messrs: H.A. Allen, Howard Davis, Ernest Dumbleton, Grahame Farr, Alfred Harvey, Cyril Hawkins Garrington, John Graham, Jim Hendry, Edwin Keen, Victor Keen, Graham Langmuir, Ernest Nurse, Eric Payne, Fred Plant, Dr R.V.C. Richards, Capt. L.G.A. Thomas. Ernest Vivian Tucker, Will Widden, Howard Woodberry.

The following employees of P&A Campbell Ltd:
Peter Southcombe (Former Traffic Manager).
The late Messrs Fred Birmingham and his son Fred P. Birmingham (Ilfracombe Agents), Alexander Campbell, (Chief Engineer – Capt. Peter's son), Capt. Henry Chidgey, Ernest Dumbleton, Bill Forbes (Purser), Jack Guy and William E. James (Traffic Managers), J.W.J. Jenkins (Company Secretary), John MacGregor and Albert E. Prince (Marine Superintendents), James Martin, (Chief Officer), Capt. Albert V. Murphy, Capt. Frederick Nunn, Capt. William Riddell, Capt. Duncan Smith, Sydney Smith-Cox, (sometime Managing Director), Arthur E. Smyth, (Swansea Agent), Alec Taylor, (Purser), John Taylor, (Chief Engineer), Capt. Daniel Taylor, Walter Vickery, (Purser), Capt. E.J. Wide.

Ilfracombe Pier Staff:
The late: Fred Comer, Capt. Claude Irwin, (Harbourmaster), Samuel Morman, (Signalman), Fred Rudd, John "Tug" Wilson, (Harbour Constable).

Ilfracombe Residents:
Mrs Joy Slocombe, (Former Curator of Ilfracombe Museum). The late Messrs: Mervyn G. Palmer FRGS, (Curator of Ilfracombe Museum), Charles Thornley, (Secretary of Ilfracombe Museum), Mr & Mrs J.L. Verney, Mr J. Cutcliffe and Mrs Slade of the St. James's Place post office, H.N. Percival, Bill Stephens and his brother R.J. Stephens, Nathaniel Stephens.

The photographs in this volume are from the combined collections of Chris Collard and the late George Owen. In many cases it has been impossible, despite every effort, to establish the exact identity of the photographers. It has been considered prudent, therefore, in the interests of accuracy, not to credit the photographs individually, but to acknowledge those photographers whose work is known to be included in this volume. With regard to the photographs of unknown origins, the author apologises if any copyright has been inadvertently infringed, and hopes that this 'omnibus' acknowledgement will serve as an appreciation of all those people in recognition of their work and their invaluable contribution to this history.

Photographers:
Bristol – Garrett; M.J. Ridley; Stephens; John York. Newport – William Clifton; Huxtable Brothers; G.W. Wilson. Barry – Heber Shirvington. Ilfracombe – Batten; Catford; Phillpse & Lees; Twiss Brothers; Vickery Brothers. Rothesay – J. Adamson & Sons; Gourock – W. Robertson. South Coast – S.G. Chrimes; W.A. Pelly.

OTHER TITLES BY CHRIS COLLARD

Published by Tempus Publishing Ltd, The Mill, Brimscombe Port, Stroud, Gloucestershire, GL5 2QG:

On Admiralty Service – P&A Campbell Steamers in the Second World War.
White Funnels – The Story of Campbell Steamers 1946–1968.
P&A Campbell Pleasure Steamers 1887–1945.
P&A Campbell Pleasure Steamers from 1946.
Bristol Channel Shipping – The Twilight Years.
Bristol Channel Shipping Remembered.
P&A Campbell Steamers – The Victorian Era.

In preparation:
A Bristol Channel Album.

Published by Wheelhouse Books, 4 Ty Mawr Close, Rumney, Cardiff, CF3 3BU:

Special Excursions – The Story of Campbells Steamers 1919–1939.
A Dangerous Occupation – A Story of Paddle Minesweepers in the First World War.

Glen Avon *at the Landing Stage, Newport, during the firs few days of commencing service. July 1912*

Introduction

This book is the last of six volumes of White Funnel Fleet history from 1887 to 1968 and the second of two volumes dealing specifically with the years prior to the First World War.

The death of my good friend Herbert George Owen at the age of ninety-one in March 2003 brought an end to many years of combined research into P&A Campbell matters. He was, I believe, the last of a generation of enthusiasts who could speak with first-hand knowledge of the steamers from the 1920s. Furthermore, when his interest flourished during his schooldays there still remained many people with vivid memories of the steamers in their halcyon days before the First World War. George spoke at length to those people and meticulously recorded their recollections in numerous notebooks, which now constitute a unique archive. That particular branch of his research, however, pales in comparison with the wealth of information which he obtained from other sources over a period of nearly seventy years. Some idea of the enormous breadth of his pursuit of factual detail can be gained from the Sources and Acknowledgements sections of this volume.

George was a quiet, modest and very private person, known by name to many from his numerous contributions to shipping magazines and periodicals. He was also well known, by correspondence, to fellow enthusiasts, many of whom he never met in person. Anyone who wrote to him would, without doubt, receive a courteous reply, but he was not averse to pointing out to the authors of inaccurate historical statements, in no uncertain terms, the error of their ways.

He was scrupulously painstaking in his research and often went to extraordinary lengths to prove or disprove even the smallest detail. In a letter written to me shortly after we first met in 1960 he stated:

As the years pass by, and the number of persons fully conversant with the Campbell steamers steadily decreases, so, in like ratio, does the amount of myth and legend increase! Over the years some surprisingly inaccurate statements – one might even say inventive – have been made. These, having been repeated by later writers, are, lamentably now accepted as fact. When one is committing history to paper there can be no substitute for the most thorough and accurate research!

For over thirty years we worked together on the compilation of the pre-1914 history of P&A Campbell Ltd and the company's rival fleets. He entrusted to me, however, the honour of combining our researches and of transposing them into narrative form. It has been a mammoth task, but one which I have undertaken with great pleasure.

Much of the history in this volume is a continuation of the complex developments of that of the Victorian era recounted in the previous volume. The traumatic events which accompanied Peter and Alec Campbell's arrival in the Bristol Channel had ended, and their competitors had been defeated. Their expanding fleet of luxurious and well-maintained vessels, a high standard of catering and an efficient network of services had ensured the enthusiastic support of the public and continually rising passenger figures.

A venture on the Hampshire coast had not been favourable but the company, with its characteristic determination, was about to enter a new field of enterprise based on the Sussex coast – an association which attained considerable success and continued for many years.

For several years Bristol Channel matters were dominated by the Barry Railway and its fleet of Red Funnel steamers. Once again P&A Campbell Ltd encountered fierce competition, not only on the waters of the Bristol Channel but also in the law courts. The episode ended in ignominy for the railway and paved the way for the Campbell fleet's entry into its finest era, the Golden Years before the First World War.

THE MOVE TO SUSSEX

1878 - 1901

The 1902 season at Southampton and Southsea was so entangled with the same season at Brighton that a brief history of the Brighton, Worthing & South Coast Steamboat Co. Ltd. must be related in order to present a clear picture of the events which lead P&A Campbell Ltd into its long association with sailings on the Sussex coast.

The pages of history must be turned back to 19 September 1887 when James Lee, a tailor and outfitter of Brighton, bought fifty-six shares in the little wooden-walled paddle steamer *Brighton*. Lee, who was stated to have had some seafaring experience, although it has not been discovered in what capacity, became managing owner.

The *Brighton*, about the size of a large tug, had been running short trips from Brighton since 1878 and Lee continued this service in 1888 in company with a similar but slightly larger chartered steamer, the *May*. The latter ran coastal trips to Eastbourne and Hastings and occasionally to Ryde. It was obviously a successful season, for Lee, in the autumn of 1888, persuaded the Worthing Pier Co. to build a new landing stage, promising in return to run a steamer regularly between Brighton and Worthing.

The *May* was unavailable for the 1889 season so Lee chartered the *Queen of the Bay*, a former Blackpool steamer, built in 1867, which had later spent ten years running from Penzance to the Isles of Scilly before a brief spell in the Bristol Channel. After running for Lee in 1889 she again returned to the Bristol Channel where she was chartered principally to Edwards, Robertson & Co. before being destroyed by fire at Liswerry Pill in the river Usk on 22 May 1894.

In 1890 James Lee again chartered the *May* and enjoyed another successful season. So much so that it aroused the interest of the residents of Brighton and Hove, leading to the formation, on 23 January 1891, of the Brighton, Worthing & South Coast Steamboat Co. Ltd, with Lee as its managing director and secretary. The company then purchased the former Clyde steamer, *Adela*, which was delivered to Shoreham harbour in May 1891. The *Adela*'s name was changed to *Sea Breeze* and during the summer of 1891 she operated in conjunction with James Lee's privately owned *Brighton*.

Brighton *on the South Coast during the 1880s.*

Queen of the Bay *in Penzance harbour in the early 1880s.*

Adela *at an unknown location in the Firth of Clyde in the 1880s.*

Princess May *on trials in the Firth of Clyde. 27 April 1893.*

In November 1891 Lee sat and passed the Board of Trade examination for a Home Trade Master's Certificate of Competency. He sold the *Brighton* to the Brighton & Worthing Co. in April 1892 and after another successful season the company ordered a new steamer from Barclay & Curle & Co. of Glasgow.

This vessel was 160ft long by 21.5ft beam and was launched on 7 April 1893 as the *Princess May*. Her trials took place on 27 April, not on the Skelmorlie measured mile but between the 'Lights', (Cloch to Cumbrae and return), achieving a mean speed of 14 knots.

She arrived at the West Pier, Brighton, on 4 May and began her season four days later. The *Brighton* had already commenced her sailings but the *Sea Breeze* did not run for the Brighton company during the 1893 season. As detailed in the previous volume she was laid up in Shoreham Harbour until being chartered by P&A Campbell Ltd for the Cardiff to Weston service.

The *Princess May* continued to run with the little *Brighton* for the 1894 and 1895 seasons but in 1896 the Brighton Co. was faced with intense competition from the *Plymouth Belle*. This steamer had been built in 1895 by John Scott & Co. of Kinghorn for the Plymouth Belle Steamship Co. of Plymouth, who had employed her on three-day excursions to the Channel Islands and the Isles of Scilly. The season having proved un-remunerative, she was chartered by Richard Ragsdale Collard of Hastings who placed her on the Brighton station. The *Plymouth Belle* was a very much larger and more up to date vessel than the *Princess May,* being 220ft long by 26ft beam and was at that date the only paddle steamer on the South Coast plated up to the bows with a continuous promenade deck.

She commenced sailing from Brighton on 1 June 1896 with a trip to Eastbourne and Hastings, and began her Boulogne trips on 5 June. Collard also chartered another small steamer, the *Nelson*, which he placed at Brighton, fiercely competing with the *Brighton* by offering identical short trips at the same times.

Whether the Brighton Co. had advanced information of Collard's intentions regarding Brighton or whether they were already contemplating ordering new tonnage is not known, but in June 1896 they received two tenders from J.&G. Thomson of Clydebank. One was for £24,100 and the other £34,400; neither was accepted.

Meanwhile, the Brighton Co. chartered John Gunn's *Lorna Doone* as some measure towards combating the *Plymouth Belle*. She arrived in Shoreham, from the Bristol Channel, on 3 July 1896, under the command of the notorious Capt. Nathan Hucker, and made her first trip from Brighton on 6 July to Eastbourne. As she had no No.2 Certificate she was unable to cross the channel and was restricted to coastal trips visiting Eastbourne, Hastings and Dover, and westward to Shanklin and Southampton.

Eventually, the Brighton Co., after much hesitation, signed a contract for the building of a new steamer with the Clydebank Shipbuilding & Engineering Co. Ltd, (formerly J.&G. Thomson), on 15 January 1897. She was to be 240ft long by 28ft beam and 10ft depth, at a cost of £25,750. Delivery was to be not later that 15 June

Princess May *entering Newhaven harbour in the 1890s.*

Plymouth Belle *on the Sussex coast in 1896. The paddle steamer in the background is the* Alexandra.

1897; the usual progress payments were to be made and the balance of the contract price was to be paid within two years of delivery, with interest at 4 per cent on the amount unpaid after delivery; any monies still unpaid by 15 June 1899 to bear thereafter an interest rate of 10 per cent.

Plymouth Belle *arriving at Eastbourne in the 1890s.*

Nelson *off Brighton in the late 1890s.*

Lorna Doone *leaving Bournemouth in the late 1890s.*

During the winter of 1898/99 the Lorna Doone *was taken into the yard of J. Samuel White & Co. Ltd of Cowes for an extensive engine overhaul and re-boiling. Three new boilers were fitted, two abreast, forward, the uptakes leading into the existing funnel, while the third was abaft these and required an extra funnel. However, proving exceptionally 'hungry' for coal, her furnaces were reduced in the winter of 1899/1900 and the second funnel, no longer required, was removed in the following winter. In the photograph above, the smoke-blackened top of the after funnel indicates that it was taken in 1899, when the after boiler was in use. In the photograph overleaf, showing her approaching Clarence Pier, Southsea, the after funnel is perfectly clean and indicates that it was taken in 1900.*

Lorna Doone *approaching Clarence Pier, Southsea, in 1900.*

The steamer was built under Board of Trade survey and construction was superintended by Capt. Lee. Many of his ideas were said to have been incorporated in her, including a bow rudder, bilge keels and nine watertight compartments. She was launched from the Clydebank yard on 20 May 1897 as the *Brighton Queen*, and proved to be a remarkably fine vessel, extremely well built. Her official trials were run on 15 June 1897 when she attained a mean speed of 18.44 knots on the measured mile at Skelmorlie.

Her promenade deck was continuous, except for the rope handling space aft. Two deck saloons, with large plate glass windows, were fitted to the main deck fore and aft of the boiler and machinery spaces; the saloons, however, were remarkably small, measuring 16ft wide with 6ft alleyways either side. The main deck, from the bulwarks up, was open, the promenade deck above being supported by stanchions. The only plating from the main deck up was a short section in the bows, and that forming the sponson houses. The sponson bulwarks were the usual Thomson style, only 3ft 6in high, with doors to the knuckle, an arrangement which was to give no little trouble during her first season.

The forward bridge had an enclosed wheelhouse with glass windows which contained only the steering wheel, binnacle and compass and one engine room telegraph. The after bridge amidships extended thwartships to the inboard faces of the paddle boxes and was used for conning the ship at piers, the engine room and docking telegraphs being situated here. A catwalk on the starboard side connected the two bridges. Her compound diagonal engines were supplied with steam from a double-ended return-tube boiler working under forced draught with uptakes leading into one funnel.

Above, below and overleaf: Brighton Queen *fitting out at John Brown's yard, Clydebank, June 1897.*
(National Archives of Scotland. Ref UCS1/119/306/1).

(National Archives of Scotland. Ref UCS1/119/306/2).

(National Archives of Scotland. Ref UCS1/119/306/3).

The funnel colours of the Brighton & Worthing Co. had hitherto been yellow with a black top but the *Brighton Queen* wore, for her first season only, a salmon coloured funnel with a dark blue top. A cowl top was fitted; its correct name being a 'watershed', for that was its prime function, to prevent rainwater and salt spray entering between the outer and inner casings of the funnel and causing corrosion.

The paddle wheels, of American rock elm, each had seven floats, 12ft 6in wide by 3ft 6in deep by 4in thick. Two large lifeboats were carried in davits at the after end of the promenade deck, hoisted sufficiently high enough to clear the passengers' heads and a small jolly boat was slung in davits over the stern. Provision was made on the after promenade deck for an awning and the device on her paddle box was the Brighton coat of arms.

Above and below: Brighton Queen *on trials in the Firth of Clyde. 15 June 1897.*

Brighton Queen *on the South Coast in 1898.*

Brighton Queen *at Eastbourne. 1899/1901.*

The *Brighton Queen* had a very dirty passage around from her builders. Leaving Clydebank on the afternoon of Tuesday 15 June 1897, under the command of Capt. Lee, she swung her compass off Gourock and headed south. At 22.30 the light on Corsewall Point was sighted; the barometer fell sharply and the wind freshened to gale force from the south-west. At about midnight the wind suddenly veered to the north-west and blew at hurricane force causing a high sea to rise. The ship's course was then shaped for the Irish coast to obtain a lee. When about 11 miles eastward of St John's Point, heavy seas stove in both the port and starboard sponson doors and tons of water were shipped on the main deck. Speed was reduced to dead slow and after fetching St John's Point a course was set for Kingstown Harbour, (Now Dun Laoghaire). The *Brighton Queen* then had the wind abeam and rolled heavily as she steamed across Dundalk Bay towards Lambay Island. Between 02.00 and 03.00 on 16 June she felt the full force of the storm, continually shipping water, with the main deck awash.

She reached Kingstown and lay there at anchor until 04.00 on Thursday 17 June when she hove up and proceeded down the St George's Channel. At about 09.30 she passed The Smalls, off the Pembrokeshire coast, and set course for Land's End, but the wind had backed again to the south-west and soon blew a strong gale with the ship labouring heavily and having to be slowed down to 10 knots. She rounded the Longships at 21.00 and passed The Lizard at 22.30, running before mountainous seas. The Isle of Wight was sighted just before 11.00 on Friday 18 June and she docked in Newhaven Harbour at about 16.30. Her storm damage was quickly repaired and she ran her first trip on the following morning – a cruise in the channel – followed by an afternoon trip to Eastbourne. She attended the Diamond Jubilee Naval Review on 26 June 1897 and continued to run cruises around the fleet until it dispersed, before making her first trip to Boulogne on Saturday 3 July. Capt. Nathan Hucker had cast in his lot with the Brighton Co., first taking command of the *Princess May* from the beginning of the 1897 season, then transferring to the *Brighton Queen* after her arrival from the Clyde and remaining with her until the end of the 1901 season.

Richard Collard had again chartered the *Plymouth Belle* and the *Nelson* for the 1897 season but was inexplicably late starting, the first trips of the two vessels taking place as late as 14 July. He had vainly sought to charter Campbells' *Britannia* and *Westward Ho* to 'run off' the *Brighton Queen*. At a directors' meeting on 21 May 1897 Alec Campbell stated that Collard had offered £5,400 and £4,400 respectively but after a brief discussion it was decided that it would be short sighted to let them go.

During the winter of 1897/1898 alterations were made to the *Brighton Queen*. It had been found that seas breaking over the low sponson bulwarks in bad weather continually flooded the main deck, so the sponsons were plated in from the houses to the ship's sides. Another problem had been caused by her stockless anchors, the hawsepipes being so close to the waterline that every time the ship pitched in a head sea the anchors threw a shower of heavy spray which was blown inboard over the foredeck and bridge windows; the indraught through the open foredeck also sucked in heavy spray to the main deck. To cure this problem the hawsepipes were raised and a catting davit was fitted in the bow, the anchors being stowed inboard on deck.

Ruby, (*ex*-Alexandra, *ex*-Aquila), *arriving at Deal in the 1890s.*

The *Sussex Daily News* of 17 April 1898 announced that during the 1897 season the *Brighton Queen* had steamed over 10,000 miles and had carried over 147,000 passengers, but nothing was mentioned about any profit having been made. On 15 June 1898 the Brighton Co. could pay only the interest of just over £657 on the remaining £16,432 still owed on the mortgage.

Nevertheless, competition from the *Brighton Queen* appears to have been too much for Richard Collard who chartered neither the *Plymouth Belle* nor the *Nelson* in 1898, but, instead, chartered the *Ruby,* (ex-*Alexandra*, ex-*Aquila*), for the month of August only. The *Plymouth Belle,* however, was back at Brighton in 1898, this time on charter to South Coast & Continental Steamers Ltd of Southampton. No doubt the company though it wiser to work the Sussex coast rather than to attempt to compete with the *Cambria* and *Lorna Doone* at Southampton and Southsea, but even they could not make her pay. During the winter of 1898/1899 she was sold to the Hamburg–Amerika Line for service between Hamburg and Heligoland, under the name of *Wilkommen.*

During the same winter the *Brighton Queen* went to a London shipyard to have her after main deck plated in, with portholes. At the same time the two after lifeboats were moved to the after sponsons.

Her owners, however, were still experiencing financial difficulties. By 31 March 1899 still only the interest of just over £657 could be paid on the *Brighton Queen's* mortgage, and on 16 June the Clydebank company transferred their mortgage to the Capital & Counties Bank, London. Under the terms of the agreement signed with the shipbuilders all monies unpaid after 15 June 1899 were to bear the increased rate

Worthing Belle *on the South Coast in the 1900s.*

of 10 per cent so the Brighton Co. now had to find approximately £1,640 interest per annum.

July 1900 saw, once again, only the interest on the *Brighton Queen's* mortgage being paid. For July and August the Brighton Co. chartered the *Jupiter*, (ex-*Lord of the Isles*), and although advertised as 'The Company's Magnificent Saloon Cross Channel Steamer' she was confined to coastal trips only, not having a No.2 Certificate.

Meanwhile, in January 1900 Capt. James Lee had a dispute with his directors which led to his resignation from the Brighton Co. In February 1901, however, he decided to compete with his old company and bought the North British Steam Packet Co.'s paddle steamer, *Diana Vernon*, renaming her *Worthing Belle*.

It has often been stated that Capt. Lee also bought, in 1901, the *Tantallon Castle* from the Galloway Saloon Steam Packet Co. Ltd of Leith, (a subsidiary of the North British Steam Packet Co.). This was not so. The *Tantallon Castle* was sold to Capt. Walter Hawthorn, Master Mariner, of London, for £15,250, the bill of sale being made out on 23 May 1901. This vessel was destined to experience many changes of ownership and name, and was eventually to ply in the Bristol Channel, and later join the White Funnel Fleet.

The *Tantallon Castle* had been built for the Galloway Co. by John Scott & Co. of Kinghorn at a cost of £15,686. She was launched with steam up on 6 May 1899, this being standard practice in Scott's yard. At 210ft long she was the largest ship yet built for the Galloway Co. and possessed some unusual features. Her two very tall funnels were oval shaped, rare at that date, and were fitted with cowl tops: her two lifeboats were slung in davits abreast of one another on the quarter deck aft: the companionways from the main deck to the promenade deck were not amidships but fore and aft of the paddle boxes on either side, whereby much useful space in the sponson houses was wasted: her bridge was amidships spanning the paddle boxes: the saloons fore and aft were provided with large glass windows but the foredeck was open. Her interior fittings were opulent and ornate with much carved oak and walnut; even stained glass windows adorned the after end of the main saloon.

It appears obvious that a previous arrangement had been made between Capt. Hawthorn and Capt. Lee regarding the running of the steamer, as she was renamed *Sussex Belle* by Board of Trade minute on the same date as that of her sale. She ran in conjunction with the *Worthing Belle* with Lee as her master for the 1901 season. He also managed her, but had no share in her ownership.

There can be little doubt that the two 'Belles' made serious inroads into the Brighton Co.'s coastal takings. Additionally, the completion of the new pavilion on Brighton's Palace Pier attracted many visitors and helped to swell the number of passengers. Capt. Lee had initiated trips to and from Littlehampton and Bognor, an innovation which became very popular, and the *Sussex Belle* frequently visited Shanklin and Southampton.

Capt. Lee made an attempt to charter the *Cambria* for several days in August and September to run to Boulogne as the *Sussex Belle* was without a No.2 Certificate, (despite referring to her in his advertisement as a 'cross channel' steamer), but was able to obtain her for one day only – Sunday 18 August 1901 – to view a Religious Festival at Boulogne.

Towards the end of 1901 Walter Hawthorn found himself in financial difficulties. He had mortgaged the *Sussex Belle* twice. Both mortgagees transferred the mortgages to the notorious Joseph Constant who, as was his 'speciality', foreclosed them both and seized the ship, selling her again on the same day to Frederick Coxhead who formed the Sussex Steam Packet Co. Ltd, Constant himself providing a mortgage for Coxhead. Capt. Hawthorn was appointed manager and became master of the *Sussex Belle*. Capt. Lee now formed a new company – Lee Ltd. – and continued to operate the *Worthing Belle*.

The Brighton Co. was also in trouble. Over recent years there had been a number of changes of directors and a serious disagreement appears to have taken place toward the end of the year which brought matters to a head on 20 December 1901, when an extraordinary General Meeting of the shareholders was held at the Royal Pavilion, Brighton. A resolution was passed whereby the company, owing to its liabilities, was to be wound up and that its three ships, the *Brighton*, *Princess May* and *Brighton Queen* were to be put up for sale.

Tantallon Castle *on trials in the Firth of Forth. June 1899.*

Sussex Belle *in Newhaven harbour in the early 1900s.*

1902

Alec and Peter Campbell cast covetous eyes on the *Brighton Queen* and began negotiations for her purchase. They were certainly not interested in the *Brighton* and they did not want the *Princess May*, but one point on which the liquidators were adamant was that both the *Brighton Queen* and the *Princess May* were to be sold together. The *Brighton Queen* was too good a ship to pass by so both vessels were purchased privately by Peter and Alec on 26 February 1902. They were bought with a mortgage from Guybon Hutson and it was only at this late date that the balance of the Brighton Co.'s original mortgage on the ship was discharged.

The *Brighton* was sold to Capt. Nathan Hucker, he knowing only too well that he would never secure employment with the Campbell brothers.

The *Brighton Queen* left Shoreham on 27 February 1902 and arrived in the Queen's Dock, Glasgow, on 3 March. Hutson's had the job of reconstruction but sub-contracted the work to John Shearer & Sons next door at the Kelvinhaugh.

The alterations were extensive and cost £6,000. The top half of the wheelhouse and its after end were removed leaving an open bridge, Campbell fashion. The engine room and docking telegraphs were shifted from the after bridge to the fore bridge. The beams of the wings of the after bridge were left to stand as awning spreaders and a ladder on the port side gave access for passengers. A canvas dodger was fitted around the fore end of the top of the after bridge converting the whole into a 'reserved deck', for which an extra charge of 6*d* was made.

New paddle wheels were fitted, now having eight floats instead of seven, of the same dimensions as the originals but made of steel, curved and flanged as in the

Brighton Queue *and* Princess May *off Brighton in 1898.*

Britannia. New wing houses were built with new sponsons and new paddle box faces, fan shaped, again Campbell fashion.

It was below deck that massive alterations were made. Plans submitted to the Board of Trade confirm that it was the Campbell brothers who had the after saloon extended to the full width of the hull and the full length of the after end of the ship. The mainmast was lifted out as it obstructed the entrance to the saloon by passing through the decks, and a ladies cabin was fitted on the port side of the saloon entrance.

The dining saloon was removed to the lower deck. By permission of the Board of Trade, (which would certainly never be granted today), two of the nine watertight bulkheads were cut through to give sufficient space for the dining saloon, but below the deck of this saloon the bulkheads were left intact. The open foredeck was plated in, with portholes, the stanchions having to be removed and replaced with new frames which were scarphed to the old ones from the main deck up.

Capt. Dan Taylor was in Glasgow supervising the alterations at Shearer's yard. At the same time Capt. Peter was staying with his sister, Isabella, at Blairmore and travelled frequently by steamer to Glasgow to see how the job was progressing.

Whitsun of 1902 was early; Whit Sunday falling on 18 May. The *Cambria*, under the command of Capt. John West, went south on 14 May and ran her first trip, on Saturday 17 May, from Southampton and South Parade Pier to Sandown, Shanklin, Ventnor and towards The Needles.

Peter and Alec Campbell, (not the limited company), opened an office at 70 Ship Street, Brighton, and engaged Mr Richard Frith Beard, formerly of the Brighton & Worthing Co., as their agent. They were now faced with a problem. In addition to running from Southampton and Southsea they had to contrive to keep the Brighton station open until the arrival of the *Brighton Queen,* for the *Brighton, Sussex Belle,* and *Worthing Belle* were running unopposed. To compound matters the new Victoria Pier at Cowes had been opened on 26 March 1902 and the Campbell brothers naturally wished the *Cambria* to call there regularly.

A carefully integrated programme was devised which not only provided as comprehensive a service as possible for both areas, but also minimised wasteful light running between resorts.

The *Brighton Queen,* tastefully painted in Campbells' colours, left the Queen's Dock, Glasgow, for Greenock on Saturday 14 June 1902. She ran her trials on the Skelmorlie mile on the morning of Monday 16 June, flying the Campbell brothers' new pendant – light blue with a white St George's Cross with a letter 'C', also in blue, in the centre of the cross. Her trials speed averaged 19 knots, with the best run being 19.5 knots. After returning to Greenock she coaled and sailed at 18.45 with Peter Campbell in command and Dan Taylor as mate. She passed The Lizard just after 22.30 on Tuesday 17 June, ran into fog which slowed her down for a while, and arrived at Southampton at 09.45 on Wednesday 18 June. Capt. Allan Livingstone then took over the *Cambria,* allowing Capt. John West to take command of the *Brighton Queen,* which ran her first trip from Brighton, to Shanklin, on Saturday 21 June 1902.

Above and below: Brighton Queen *on trials in the Firth of Clyde for Peter and Alec Campbell. Monday 16 June 1902.*

The Coronation Naval Review for King Edward VII was to take place on Saturday 28 June 1902 and Alec Campbell had made great preparations for the event. An advertisement by the South Parade Pier Co. in the *Portsmouth Evening News* on Saturday 21 June stated:

The Best Steamers run from The South Parade Pier. Frequent Excursions to view the Fleet - Southwold Belle, Duke of Devonshire, Princess May, Cambria and Brighton Queen. Fare 1/-. First trip 10am on Monday 23 June.

Princess May *in the Merchant's Dock, Bristol, awaiting her refit. March 1902.*

The *Princess May* had sailed from Shoreham and Southampton, and arrived in Bristol on 9 March 1902. Her refit consisted of minor alterations only; the Campbell brothers not being disposed to spend a great deal of time or money on her, other than her being painted in the fleet's colours. Incidentally, both the *Brighton Queen* and the *Princess May* had been fitted with naval type sirens in addition to the usual steam whistles. The *Brighton Queen* retained hers but that of the *Princess May* was mounted on the funnel of the *Cambria* and remained there to the end of her days.

The *Princess May* made a number of experimental trips in the Bristol Channel, mainly between Cardiff and Weston, but proved to be not only too small, but often hard-pressed to contend with the fast flowing tides. Under the command of Capt. Neil McLeod she left Bristol for Southampton on Thursday 19 June – it has been claimed on charter – but this appears to have been merely an arrangement with the South Parade Pier Co. to run exclusively from their pier for the period of the review, according to the above advertisement

The *Britannia* was to leave Bristol on Thursday 26 June at 09.30, calling at Cardiff, Penarth and Ilfracombe, due to arrive at Bournemouth at 08.00 on the following day. On the Saturday – Review Day – she was to leave Bournemouth Pier at 10.00 to cruise around the fleet, returning from Bournemouth to Bristol at 11.00 on Monday 30 June. The fare was three guineas.

Refitted, and painted in Campbell colours, the Princess May *enters the Cumberland Basin lock. 1902.*

Princess May *in the Cumberland Basin. 1902.*

A special train was to leave Cardiff Riverside station for Barry Pier, thence by the *Lady Margaret* to Burnham, where another train would be waiting to convey passengers to Bournemouth. Trains were also scheduled to leave Newport at 04.00 on Review Day to connect with the Barry train at Cardiff Riverside. The *Cambria* and the *Westward Ho* were to have run from Bournemouth to connect with the rail excursions, the combined fare for which, from either Cardiff or Newport, was two guineas

The *Brighton Queen* ran from Brighton every day from Monday 23 June, calling at Southsea, and steamed through the lines of assembling warships. On Review Day she was to sail from Newhaven, via the Palace and West Piers, Brighton, for Spithead.

Unfortunately King Edward was taken ill with appendicitis and although he was operated on successfully on Wednesday 24 June, the review had to be postponed. The Campbells, however, advertised 'The boats will run the advertised trips', with the exception of the *Westward Ho*, which does not appear to have gone around from Bristol.

After the fleet had dispersed on Wednesday 2 July, the *Princess May* continued to run short trips between Southsea, Ryde, Cowes and Southampton. She had, however, attracted the attention of representatives of an Italian company – Societa di Navigazione a Vapore della Penisola Sorrentina, of Castellamare – who began successful negotiations for her purchase. As she was not owned by the limited company, no details of the sale appear in the minute books.

The *Princess May* had an easy passage to Naples, leaving Southampton on Tuesday 31 July. She was at Gibraltar on 6 August and arrived at her destination on 12 August, when she took her new name of *Principessa Jolanda*. She was sold to another Neapolitan owner in 1907 and then in 1908 to Serafina Vassilieva of Odessa. She continued to be listed in Lloyds' Register as *Principessa Jolanda* until 1914/1915 when it read 'Now renamed *Vasilieff*'. She disappeared from Lloyds' Register in 1929.

The *Brighton Queen* made her first trip from Brighton to Boulogne under Campbell ownership on Monday 14 July 1902. On the same day the *Cambria* made her first trip of the season to Cherbourg. She left Southampton at 07.15 with a large party from Birmingham who had travelled down by rail overnight and who breakfasted aboard.

The two steamers then began alternating their destinations. In addition to her Boulogne sailings, the *Brighton Queen* made trips westward to the Hampshire resorts, the Isle of Wight and to Swanage, while the *Cambria,* in addition to her Solent and Cherbourg trips, journeyed to the Sussex resorts and to Boulogne. All went well until Bank Holiday Monday 4 August. The *Western Mail* takes up the story:

Nearly 200 persons had an experience on Monday which they had not arranged for in their holiday programme. They had boarded the Brighton Queen on her trip to

Boulogne, had seen as much as possible on the other side of the channel, and in the late afternoon started on the return journey. The evening was delightful and the passengers whiled away the time in singing or in seasickness. Those who were on deck saw the lights along the front at Hastings twinkling like stars as the steamer made good speed for the pier. All at once there was a harsh grating – the vessel had struck on the rocks some distance off Hastings. Immediately there was tremendous excitement amongst the passengers. Some of the women found an unsafe refuge in tears, while those who were seasick and desiring death five minutes before suddenly lost that longing in anticipation that the boat might sink.

The *Brighton Queen* had had the misfortune to ground on a patch known as 'Castle Rock'. The tide was at half flood so she came off easily after a short time but was found to be making water. Her pumps were started and she made fast at Hastings Pier where all of her passengers were hurried ashore. Arrangements were then made to return them to their destinations by train.

Meanwhile, the *Brighton Queen*, very much down by the head and with her pumps working hard, arrived at Newhaven at 23.00, where the harbour master and eight men had turned out to put her on to the gridiron. As soon as she had drained, her bottom damage was cemented and she left Newhaven for Southampton where she arrived at 04.20 on Wednesday 6 August, immediately entering dry dock for survey.

The surveyor's report stated:

> *Brighton Queen* has considerable damage involving about 30 shell plates. Find heavy internal damage, 55 floors and frames broken, also keelsons and several bulkhead plates damaged. Repairs will necessitate lifting heavy double ended boiler and removing portion of auxiliary machinery.

It was obvious that the *Brighton Queen* would be out of service for a considerable time. This was extremely unfortunate; the loss of earning power during August Bank Holiday week, the busiest week of the year, being further aggravated by the postponed Naval Review looming up. Alec immediately asked permission of the directors to substitute the *Cambria* at Brighton until the *Brighton Queen* was able to return to service. He stated that the Brighton sailings were far more remunerative than those from Southampton and that as the *Albion* would be working out of Southampton during review week, she would be available to take the *Cambria*'s ordinary running in the meantime. The directors agreed, and the *Albion*, having concluded her Bank Holiday week's work in the Bristol Channel, arrived at Southampton on the evening of Sunday 10 August.

Once again the warships were assembling for the review, now scheduled for Saturday 16 August 1902. The *Albion*, under the command of Capt. J.H. Denman with Capt. John West as pilot, began her trips around the fleet on Monday 11 August, while the *Cambria* performed similar trips from Brighton.

Above and below: Brighton Queen *on the gridiron in Newhaven harbour on Tuesday 5 August 1902, undergoing temporary repairs following her grounding on Castle Rock, off Hastings, on the previous evening.*

Cambria *in Southampton Water in the early 1900s.*

Heather Bell *in the river Avon in 1902.*

The *Britannia* again went to Spithead, leaving Bristol at 13.30 on Thursday 14 August, via Cardiff, Penarth and Ilfracombe. On the morning of Review Day she sailed from Bournemouth for a cruise through the fleet prior to anchoring for the review, after which she returned to Bournemouth to embark passengers for an evening cruise to see the illuminations. On Monday 18 August, before returning to Bristol in the evening, she followed the warships to sea and witnessed a staged sea battle; unfortunately the latter event was marred by strong winds. The review sailings of the *Cambria* and *Albion* had followed a similar pattern.

The *Brighton Queen* re-entered service on Wednesday 3 September. Capt. West again took command of her; Capt. Denman, in the *Albion,* having the services of Capt. Neil McLeod as pilot for the rest of her season.

The *Cambria* returned to Bristol, carrying passengers from Southampton and Bournemouth, on Friday 26 September. The *Albion,* unadvertised and not carrying passengers, left Southampton for Bristol on Tuesday 30 September. The *Brighton Queen* sailed from Brighton on the morning of Friday 3 October bound for Bristol. She discharged her passengers on arrival, bunkered and sailed immediately for the Queen's Dock, Glasgow, where she was to spend the winter.

In the Bristol Channel the 1902 season had progressed with little incident. The *Heather Bell* once again provided some competition, particularly against the *Bonnie Doon* out of Newport. That season the hull of the *Heather Bell* was painted black, the Bristol pilots having complained in 1901 that her grey hull made her difficult to see in the Avon during hazy or foggy weather. If her hull was not clearly seen her funnel was – yellow with a black top and a red band with a large 'H' in blue on either side! Her two seasons appear to have been somewhat un-remunerative. Edwin Hunt sold her to Dutch ship-breakers in the spring of 1903. The tug *Hollandia* came to Bristol to tow her away and she was reported as having passed Ventnor on 1 May 1903 bound for Rotterdam.

1903

At the P&A Campbell director's meeting on 19 December 1902 the secretary read a telegram from a shipbroker, acting on behalf of the same company which had bought the *Princess May,* offering to buy the *Scotia.* Negotiations followed and on 15 January 1903 the *Scotia* was sold to Societa di Navigazione a Vapore della Penisola Sorrentina for £5050.

Unlike the *Princess May,* the *Scotia* had a dirty passage to Naples. She left Bristol on 22 January 1903 but had to shelter at Ilfracombe for three days and then for another two days in the lee of Lundy. She had to shelter again in Falmouth, not sailing from there until 3 February. She put into Lisbon for coal on 9 February, passed Sagres on 14 February and arrived at Naples on 22 February, where she became *Principessa Mafalda.* She was sold again in the winter of 1906/1907 and was re-named *Epomeo,* after a mountain on the island of Ischia. The *Epomeo* was said to have been sunk by a mine near Sorrento in 1914/1915 but her Lloyds' Register entry for 1913/1914 states 'Broken up'.

Scotia leaving Ilfracombe. *1899/1903.*

The officers and crew of the Scotia *photographed at the Landing Stage, Newport, in the early 1900s. Seated centre is Capt. Hector McFadyen; on his right is Chief Officer Frederick Nunn, and on Capt. McFadyen's left is Chief Engineer Robert Wilson.*

Scotia *at anchor off*
Sorrento. 12 March 1903.

Another sale was also in the offing, Alec having reported to the directors that
representatives of the Furness Railway had visited Portishead to inspect the *Lady
Margaret*. He had quoted £17,000 as the price likely to be entertained by the board.
At the meeting on 26 January 1903 the secretary read a letter from Mr Arthur Aslett,
the general manager of the Furness Railway Co., offering £13,000. P&A Campbell
Ltd replied that they would sell for £15,000. At a further meeting on 11 February
1903 a wire was read offering £14,000. Alec pointed out that an expenditure of
£2000 to £2500 might be looked for at any time within the following few years
for a new boiler. It was decided, therefore, to accept Mr Aslett's offer.

A Furness Railway crew came to fetch the *Lady Margaret*, which left Bristol on
27 March 1903. A heavy westerly gale forced her to shelter in Penarth Roads until
08.00 on 31 March, but once under way she made a good passage, arriving off Piel
Island at 04.00 on 1 April.

With Mount Vesuvius just visible in the distance and the former Clyde paddle steamer Galatea *in the background, the* Principessa Mafalda, (ex-Scotia), *lies in Naples harbour.*

Lady Margaret *arriving at Penarth, 1896/1902.*

Lady Margaret *at Fleetwood during her Furness Railway days.*

Brighton Queen *in Portishead Dock in May 1903.*

Alec had reported to the directors, on 3 November 1902, that the results of the season's trading from Southampton had not been satisfactory. He added that if the board decided not to send the *Cambria* south for the following season he thought that by means of his and his brother's steamer, the *Brighton Queen*, he might be able to 'cover her withdrawal' – a very broad hint! The matter was discussed at several meetings which eventually led to Peter and Alec selling the *Brighton Queen* to the limited company on 7 May 1903.

A number of alterations had been carried out during the winter months including the refurbishment of the forward saloon and the installation of large electric fans to improve ventilation in the dining saloon. The *Brighton Queen* left Glasgow on 17 May 1903 and docked in Portishead on the following day.

On 19 May the Campbell shareholders were given a complimentary trip, leaving Hotwells at 09.30 in the *Westward Ho* to join the *Brighton Queen* at Clevedon. Having called at Penarth to pick up shareholders from the Cardiff district she cruised down the Welsh coast as far as Nash Point, then across to Lynmouth and back up-channel on the Devon and Somerset side before returning to Penarth and Clevedon, where the Bristol contingent disembarked to return home by train, the *Brighton Queen* again docking in Portishead.

During the cruise the shareholders were entertained to lunch, in the process of which a number of speeches were made extolling the virtues of the ship. Alec, in reply, stated that the *Brighton Queen* had been a popular steamer on the South Coast during 1902 and he hoped that in 1903 her popularity would be further increased, for it was the company's intention to make her 'the talk of the south coast of England'.

This did indeed become a fact; Alec engaged a first class chef and ensured that an excellent selection of French wines was always available. Dinner aboard the *Brighton Queen* when returning from Boulogne or Calais became famous, many passengers making the trips for the sole purpose of enjoying the excellent cuisine.

The *Brighton Queen* left Portishead for Bournemouth and Southampton on the evening of Tuesday 26 May 1903. On arrival at Southampton she was held for survey and did not make her first trip, from Brighton, until Saturday 30 May.

Several changes had taken place on the Sussex coast. Capt. Hucker had sold the *Brighton* to George Courtney, an engineer of Southwick, in whose ownership she was burnt out in Shoreham Harbour and broken up. Capt. Hucker then moved to the Thames and commanded in turn the *Koh-I-Noor* and *Royal Sovereign* until 29 April 1907 when he took the post of Piermaster at Southend-on-Sea, continuing in that capacity until his death from meningitis on 26 February 1916.

The *Sussex Belle* had also gone. Joseph Constant foreclosed on F.J. Coxhead's mortgage and seized the ship, selling her on the same day to the Colwyn Bay & Liverpool Steamship Co. who re-named her *Rhos Colwyn*. We shall, however, meet her again.

As only Capt. Lee's *Worthing Belle* was left to compete on the Brighton station, P&A Campbell Ltd sent the *Glen Rosa* to join the *Brighton Queen*, the former making her first trip from Brighton, to Shanklin, on 22 July 1903. These two steamers were to maintain the South Coast sailings for the following two years.

Brighton Queen *at Swanage in the early 1900s.*

The Campbell steamers began running to and from Worthing this year; the first call being that of the *Brighton Queen* which started her Boulogne trip from Worthing on 23 July 1903, calling at Brighton and Eastbourne. The stationing of a steamer at Southampton was abandoned from 1903 but it was still a frequent port of call on the trips to the westward and was frequently combined with the visits to Bournemouth, Swanage and the Isle of Wight resorts.

Two trips were made to Calais this season, on 27 July and 2 August. The success of the Boulogne trips continued and attracted large crowds, although many of those who boarded the *Brighton Queen* at Brighton, Eastbourne and Hastings on the morning of 20 August 1903 wished that they had stayed ashore. A violent south-westerly gale blew up very quickly and mountainous seas in the Dover Strait delayed her arrival at Boulogne until 16.00, giving her passengers a bare hour ashore. After leaving Boulogne at 17.00 and setting her course for the English coast she faced the full fury of the gale, but worse was to come. During the course of the evening the weather deteriorated and for nearly six hours she plunged and pounded violently through massive, oncoming seas. The call at Hastings was out of the question but the Eastbourne Pier staff stood by and at 22.45 they saw the lights of the *Brighton Queen* approaching. Capt. West made two attempts to berth, but the tremendous seas which were running past the pier made it impossible. She then headed back into the channel, around Beachy Head and arrived at Newhaven two and a half hours later at about 02.00 on 21 August (under normal conditions the journey would have taken her an hour). The passengers, most of who were in a most pitiable state, slept aboard and were sent home by train the following morning.

Brighton Queen *at Southampton in the early 1900s.*

Brighton Queen *at Boulogne in the early 1900s.*

Brighton Queen arriving at Eastbourne in the early 1900s.

Brighton Queen *in the river Avon in the early 1900s.*

Brighton Queen *in the Cumberland Basin in the early 1900s.*

Britannia *at Bristol in the early 1900s.*

During the period from 1897 to the end of 1902 P&A Campbell Ltd had consolidated its position on the South Coast as it had done in the Bristol Channel from 1888 to 1896. In 1903 the *Britannia* was principally engaged in running the long trips down channel from Bristol via Weston or Cardiff as well as performing the 'special' journeys, such as the weekend trip to Penzance and the Isles of Scilly which began on 3 July that year. The *Cambria* performed similar duties and was now stationed at Cardiff in place of the *Lady Margaret,* while the *Westward Ho* assisted on both routes as necessary and continued to take most of the trips down-channel from Sharpness. The *Ravenswood* and *Waverley* were the mainstays of the Cardiff to Weston ferry while the *Albion* was placed at Newport; the *Bonnie Doon* assisting on both stations.

A newcomer to the Bristol Channel brought of competition to the *Brighton* at Swansea that year when a local solicitor, Mr J.R. Richards purchased the former London, Brighton & South Coast Railway's paddle steamer *Normandy,* of 1882. This vessel, however, posed no great threat to the White Funnel Fleet, but, like the *Brighton,* of which she was a longer and improved version, became something of an 'irritation' with her trips out of Ilfracombe.

The 1903 season drew to a close with a sting in its tail when, on Friday 11 September, severe weather wrought havoc on the shores of the Bristol Channel. Hurricane force winds from the north-west washed away the greater part of Birnbeck Pier, the portion connecting Birnbeck Island with the landing stage which, although considerably damaged, remained standing. The wind and sea dealt similarly with the unfinished part of the low water pier, the construction of which had recently started on the west side of Birnbeck Island.

Weston's sea front and promenade were wrecked; streets and parks were under water; shops were flooded and many shop windows were blown in. The new electric trams running along the sea front were damaged and put out of commission.

On Friday 11 September the *Western Mail* reported:

Cyclonic Storm. Great Damage.
Passenger Steamers' Peril. Anxiety at Ilfracombe.

A telegraph from Ilfracombe, despatched at 7pm last night says – 'A heavy north-westerly gale is raging. On the pier hundreds of anxious friends are awaiting the arrival of the steamers *Normandy* and *Brighton*. The agents have wired and find that the steamers left Mumbles at about 4 o'clock, since when nothing has been heard of them and they are not in sight.' Wiring later the correspondent says that great relief was felt when the *Brighton* was observed and her passengers landed safely after a terrible passage. She reported that the *Normandy* had put back to Mumbles.

A further report appeared on the following day which stated:

The *Normandy* came alongside Ilfracombe pier this morning with about fifty passengers who had braved the heavy seas. Cheers were given by a large crowd of spectators. Capt.

A study in smoke and steam. The Westward Ho *swings on a flood tide at Bristol in the early 1900s.*

Cambria *in the Avon in the early 1900s.*

Important elements of the company's business were corporate charters. Factory outings frequently took over a ship for the whole day, as on this occasion. The Britannia, *arriving at Ilfracombe, is on charter to Cycle Components of Componentsville.*

Ravenswood *at Chepstow in the early 1900s.*

Cambria *at Chepstow in the early 1900s.*

Albion *at the Landing Stage, Newport, in the early 1900s.*

Albion *in the river Usk in the early 1900s.*

Penarth pier in the early 1900s with the Ravenswood *at the jetty and a variety of vessels, waiting to enter the Cardiff docks, in the roads.*

Brighton *arriving at Ilfracombe in the early 1900s. In the background is the* Britannia.

The severely damaged Birnbeck Pier after the gale of 11 September 1903.

Opposite above: Brighton *at anchor off Lynmouth in the early 1900s.*

Opposite below: Normandy *off Ilfracombe in the early 1900s.*

Williams said 'We left Mumbles yesterday at 4.30pm in a north westerly gale. As we crossed the Bristol Channel the gale increased to a full gale and then to hurricane force, but the ship behaved beautifully. We made land at 7.30pm, a little to the east of Ilfracombe, and then laid to, to see if the weather would moderate. Instead, it became worse and the sea on the rocks at Ilfracombe looked like a white-washed wall. I decided it was not safe to enter the port and went back to Swansea. The gale was furious but we ran into the East Dock at 10.00pm. The passengers joined us at 10am today having spent the night in an hotel ashore.'

Clevedon Pier's landing stage also suffered damage and it was not until 15 September that the steamers were able to resume calling. Weston passengers now had to travel to Clevedon and continue their journey by means of the Portishead–Clevedon–Weston Light Railway.

Despite the wet and stormy conditions which had prevailed during the 1903 season P&A Campbell Ltd were satisfied that their organisation was running smoothly and that their ships were fully utilised on the network of services which they provided. That satisfaction, however, was to be rudely shattered by the events of 1904.

The Barry Railway

1830–1904

The impact which the Barry Railway made in Bristol Channel excursion steamer circles, and on P&A Campbell Ltd in particular, was so great, so complex and so far reaching that it is necessary to digress at this point in order to provide essential background information to put matters fully into perspective.

We must retrace our steps to the 1830s when, with remarkable foresight, the second Marquis of Bute, principal landowner in Cardiff, envisaged the development of the South Wales coalfield. Seeing that the lack of accommodation for ships was the only hindrance to an immense rise in the value of his extensive tracts of mineral property, he obtained an Act of Parliament enabling him to build the Bute West Dock, which was opened in 1839. This dock cost the Marquis £350,000, an astronomical sum in those days, which swallowed up almost his entire fortune. However, the opening of the Taff Vale Railway in 1840 brought a trickle of coal down the Rhondda Valley to the Bute Dock which was eventually to swell into an overwhelming flood. Unfortunately the second Marquis died in 1848 when his heir was only one year old, leaving the Bute Estate and the Bute Docks to be administered by the Bute Trustees for the following twenty years.

By 1850 approximately 600,000 tons of coal per year was passing through the Bute Dock. A charge of 8d per ton on shipments had rapidly started money flowing into the Bute coffers and the continuing growth of coal shipments induced the Bute Trustees to build another dock – the Bute East – which was completed in 1859.

Coal from pits in both the Rhondda Fawr and Rhymney Valleys was coming down to the Cardiff Docks in ever increasing quantities. By 1860 over 2 million tons were being shipped annually, and even then congestion and lack of room in the Bute Docks was already a problem. This, however, was merely a prelude. The South Wales coalfield expanded explosively between 1873 and 1883, when output increased from 4 million tons to almost 9 million tons per year. The Bute Trustees, in 1866, had sought Parliamentary powers to build a large new dock and basin on the east side of the Bute East Dock, but Parliament would only sanction the basin, later known as the Roath Basin, opened in 1874.

While this basin was under construction the Cardiff 'Freighters' – a consortium of coal owners which included such famous names as David Davies, Archibald Hood, the Insoles and the Corys – had several discussions with John Boyle, the acting Trustee for the Marquis of Bute, stressing the lack of dock space and the congestion. Consequently the Bute Trustees went again to Parliament, proved another dock was necessary and obtained powers to construct a large new 54 acre dock. It was never built. The third Marquis, (now having attained his majority), was quite mistakenly of the opinion that the coal trade had reached its peak and that no further expansion would occur, but by 1880 coal from over 200 pits was choking the Cardiff Docks.

There was much unrest among the freighters, who were infinitely more far sighted in visualising the future expansion and development of the coal trade than Lord Bute and his Trustees. There was also much dissatisfaction with the haulage charges of the Taff Vale Railway since the coal owners of the Rhondda paid the highest rates; David Davies's Ocean Colliery alone paid the Taff Vale approximately £77,500 per year in haulage.

Matters reached a peak in 1882. Parliament agreed to Lord Bute's proposal to build a new dock, (the Roath Dock), and to increase the shipping charges by 1*d* per ton, not only at the new dock but also at all the existing Cardiff Docks. From the strong opposition of the freighters these extra charges, which would have cost them £120,000 more per year, were reduced but still meant an increase to them of £50,000 per year.

The stage was set for action by the freighters. A meeting was held at the Ocean Collieries offices in Cardiff in June 1882 to appoint engineers to report on a suitable site for a new dock. The engineers were John Wolfe Barry and H.M. Brunel, the younger son of Isambard Kingdom Brunel. On 4 July 1882 a freighters' committee met Mr Robert Forrest, the agent of the foremost landowner in Barry, Lord Windsor, who informed them that his lordship had offered to subscribe £50,000 to the scheme if Barry was chosen for the site of the new dock.

To bring in the support of the Cardiff Shipowners Association the Barry promoters approached Thomas Roe Thompson, an outstanding figure in Cardiff's dockland. A native of Sunderland, Thompson had come to Cardiff with his father and had fought his way to the top by sheer determination. Regarded as a brilliant businessman, Thompson – a shipbroker, coal exporter, pit prop importer, and already a very wealthy man – readily supported the Barry scheme, and in November 1882 the promoters signed agreements with the Barry landowners – Lord Windsor, Lord Romilly and Mr R.F.L. Jenner.

The Barry Bill was deposited in the House of Commons early in 1883, and although the preamble was proved, the intense opposition of the Bute faction induced the House of Lords Committee to throw it out. Undaunted, the Barry promoters made a further effort in the following year and after a terrific battle in Parliament lasting thirty-three days, in which David Davies's eloquence played a large part, the Bill was eventually passed by the Lords on 31 July 1884. The Barry Dock & Railway was formed with Lord Windsor as its chairman and David Davies as deputy chairman. Other directors included Archibald Hood, Edward Davies, (David Davies's son) and Thomas Roe Thompson.

Construction of the Barry Dock began in November 1884. The railway system proposed was, at first, a very modest one. The total distance authorised by the Parliamentary Bill was originally only twenty-three miles but this was to be greatly increased over the years by a multitude of Acts which the Barry company manoeuvred through Parliament – so many in fact that the Barry Co. became known as 'The spoiled child of Parliament'.

Water was first let into the 73 acres of the Barry Dock on 29 June 1889 and on 18 July the first wagon of coal thundered into the hold of the first vessel to enter, the steamer *Arno*. By the end of that year 598 ships had entered Barry and 3 million tons of coal had been exported. A dividend of 10 per cent was paid – a remarkable figure when most concerns paid 2.5 per cent to 3 per cent.

In 1891 the Barry Dock & Railway changed its name to simply the Barry Railway company. Curiously it was never a limited company.

An Act passed on 5 August 1891 provided the company with a considerable step forward. Under this Act the Taff Vale Railway was forced to grant the Barry company running powers over several of its lines so that traffic could be exchanged with the Rhymney Railway, thus providing a great new source of coal for the Barry company.

Another most important point in this Act was that the Taff Vale Railway had to provide running powers for the Barry Railway from Cogan to Penarth South Curve Junction, linking with the GWR into Cardiff. The Act also required the GWR to convert the two platforms of Cardiff Riverside station, (situated almost alongside Cardiff General station), into a passenger station for the use of both the Barry and the Taff Vale Railways. Although the Barry Railway was formed solely for handling coal, important passenger traffic also began to develop.

The line from Barry Dock station had been extended westwards to Barry Town and a further extension to Barry Island was opened on Bank Holiday Monday 3 August 1896. Furthermore, the Taff Vale Railway had made an agreement permitting the Barry company to begin passenger services between Barry, Pontypridd and Porth. Apart from obtaining running powers over as much of the Taff Vale and Rhymney Valley lines as possible, the Barry Co. took over the working of the Vale of Glamorgan Railway, which, beyond Bridgend, served the Ogmore, Llynfi and Garw Valleys. It was estimated that at holiday weekends 30,000 people or more poured into Barry Island.

Other ambitious schemes began to interest the Barry company directors. Their coal trade had increased so enormously as to necessitate the building of another new dock and by innumerable Acts they had secured running powers over almost every other railway company's lines. In fact, so successful had the Barry company become, they appeared to have considered themselves invincible.

The idea of running passenger steamers in the Bristol Channel seems to have occurred to some of the Barry directors immediately after the demise of the Cardiff steamship owners Edwards, Robertson & Co. in 1895.

At a meeting of the Campbell directors on 16 October 1895 Mr Weston stated that he had heard that it was the intention of the Barry Railway to run steamers in the channel. He remarked that this was to be regretted and suggested that prompt action on the part of P&A Campbell Ltd might be the means of inducing them to abandon the idea. The secretary was instructed to write to the secretary of the Barry Railway and ascertain if his directors would be willing to meet P&A Campbell directors to consider the suggestion of the latter company that the proposed steamer service should be carried out by the White Funnel steamers on terms to be arranged. Nothing further on this matter appeared in the Campbell minute books so one must assume that the Barry directors would not agree to the meeting.

The first press report of the Barry Railway's intentions appeared in the *South Wales Daily News*, quoting a paragraph from the *Shipping World* of September 1896:

> Several influential capitalists connected with the Barry Railway Co. are at the back of the new low water pier being constructed at Weston Super Mare. We learn on good authority that the company directors propose, next year, to establish a service of pleasure steamers between Barry and Weston, running as need requires to other holiday resorts in the Bristol Channel.

Nothing is recorded in the Barry Railway minute books until 2 April 1897 under the heading of 'Passenger Steamboat Service'. The directors Archibald Hood; T.R. Thompson; Lord Windsor's agent Robert Forrest; the Barry Railway's general manager Richard Evans and Capt. Davies, the Barry Dockmaster, were appointed a committee to consider the establishment of the steamboat services with other ports in the channel. The minute books record a further meeting, on 1 October 1897 headed 'Channel Passenger Steamers', when Hood and Thompson reported on their visits to Minehead and Wooda Bay. It was considered desirable that Messrs J.R. Davies, Benjamin Lake and Weld Blundell be asked to visit Barry Docks, and the secretary was authorised to invite them separately.

J.R. Davies was involved with the building of the new pier at Minehead, Benjamin Lake's new pier at Wooda Bay had opened in 1897, and Mr Weld Blundell was the owner of Ilfracombe Pier. No hint appeared in the minutes as to the purpose of their intended visits but it appears quite certain that the Barry directors had definitely decided, at this early date, to run their own passenger steamers in the Bristol Channel; the three great advocates being T.R. Thompson, Robert Forrest and Herbert Rees Jones (Senior).

The *Western Mail* reported on 20 November 1897 that the Barry Railway was to seek powers to provide and work steamers, and on 20 April 1898 the Barry Railway (Steam Vessels) Bill was deposited in the House of Commons.

Counsel opening the case for the promoters said that the object of the Bill was to empower the Barry Co. to subsidise steamboat companies or to become owners of steam vessels themselves. He continued by stating that immediately after the granting of an Act to extend the line from Barry Island through a tunnel to a site just west of the dock entrance, the Barry company had obtained powers to place a pontoon there for the use of steamers, and three caissons had been ordered from John Lysaght of Bristol. Counsel said that the company had almost completed the large deep-water pontoon, (which they had not – the first two caissons did not arrive until 9 June 1898 and the third

Cambria *at Wooda Bay pier, 1897.*

was much delayed), so that steamers would be able to come and go according to a fixed timetable irrespective of tides. The engineer Sir John Wolfe Barry then let the cat out of the bag by stating that it was the intention of the company to have a steamer running between Barry and Weston by way of the new low-water pier at Birnbeck Island. The chairman of the House of Commons Committee, having questioned witnesses about the low-water pier, which was only that year just started, pointed out that if there was not yet a corresponding low-water pier at Weston 'it would be like a person trying to send a telephonic message when there was no receiver at the other end'. Although the Bill was opposed by the Taff Vale Railway and P&A Campbell Ltd, their cases were not even presented; it had already failed and was duly thrown out.

T.R. Thompson, however, obtained tenders, dated 20 September 1898, from J.&G. Thomson of Clydebank. It is significant that these tenders were to T.R. Thompson and not to the Barry Railway. The tenders were for two paddle steamers 245ft by 29ft by 10ft; duplicates of the Clyde paddle steamer *Juno,* which had been built that year, and were to cost £31,000 each.

At a special meeting of the Barry board on 27 September Thompson submitted the two tenders and a long discussion followed, but having regard to the failure of the Bill it was felt that the company could not contract for the building of the two steamers. If, however, an independent company were formed for that purpose, it was in their interest to assist such an independent company by making allowances and rebates out of the bookings for passengers and goods. It was decided that a further meeting should be called especially to consider pledging the company to enter into an agreement for that purpose.

The Barry company were determined to have steamers running from Barry Pier and entered into negotiations with P&A Campbell Ltd. At a Barry company meeting on 2 December 1898 their general manager, Richard Evans, stated that Messrs Campbell were

Glen Rosa at Barry Pier in 1899.

prepared to station one boat at Barry for cross-channel traffic to Weston and, additionally, to start a steamer from Cardiff in order to leave Barry at fixed times for Ilfracombe. In the event of the tide preventing this, the steamer could lie in Barry overnight.

The Barry company stated that they required a steamer to call regularly on Wednesdays, Saturdays and the first Monday in each month; the latter being 'Mabon's Day' – the miners' holiday which had been introduced by William Abraham MP. The company also stated that they would be prepared 'to share any loss on the steamer service' – a statement which was to assume considerable significance in the light of subsequent developments.

Although the Barry company had said that the new pontoon would be ready by April 1899 it was not until 21 July that the first steamer called, when the *Lady Margaret* made a trip to Lynmouth and Ilfracombe, leaving Barry at 10.00 after the arrival of the 09.20 train from Cardiff Riverside and the 08.47 train from Pontypridd.

The *Glen Rosa* took over the Barry to Weston ferry and during the course of the 1899 season approximately 45,000 passengers were carried on the sailings out of Barry. It must be borne in mind, however, that the fare by rail from Cardiff to Barry Pier and then to Weston by steamer was 2s, the same as the steamer fare from Cardiff to Weston, but the Barry Railway took 1s 5d for the return train fare, leaving only 7d for the steamer. Similarly, the fare to Ilfracombe had 1s 5d deducted for the train fare. P&A Campbell Ltd found that at the end of the season they had lost approximately £1,000 and refused to run from Barry in 1900 unless the Barry company would make up receipts to £6,500. This the company flatly refused to do, although it will be remembered that at the Barry meeting of 2 December 1898 it was agreed that the company would be prepared to share any loss.

In early 1900 the Barry company made a second attempt to push their Steam Vessels Bill through Parliament. It came before the Select Committee on 21 March, this time opposed by the GWR and petitioned against by P&A Campbell Ltd. Meanwhile the Cardiff Chamber of Commerce had passed a resolution approving the Barry Bill. It was, however, strongly opposed by two dissentients, Mr H.J. Vellacott and Mr John Best Ferrier. The latter, a member of the Chamber and also a shareholder in the Barry Railway, opposed the resolution on the grounds that the 1899 experiment had not been successful from the shareholders point of view.

In evidence before the Select Committee T.R. Thompson stated that Messrs Campbell wanted a subsidy of £6,500, which was blatantly untrue. As already stated P&A Campbell Ltd simply asked for the receipts to be made up to that figure, thus honouring the Barry company's agreement to 'share any loss on the steamer service'.

Alec Campbell was called and stated that in his opinion the development of the Barry traffic as calculated by the promoters would not come about, the traffic was not there. If there was paying traffic from Barry his company would be delighted to supply the boats but they had found that it was only on Saturdays and bank holidays that it was worth sailing from Barry.

The Committee, having deliberated, found the Bill not proved and threw it out; the Barry company therefore finding itself without a steamer service for 1900.

T.R. Thompson obtained further tenders from John Brown & Co. Ltd, (formerly J.&G. Thomson), of Clydebank. The first was for a paddle steamer 260ft by 30ft by 10.5ft similar to the Clyde paddler *Glen Sannox,* at a cost of £41,200; the second for two paddle steamers 245ft by 29ft by 10.5ft at £35,000 each. A note in John

Glen Rosa *arriving at Weston, 1901.*

Albion *approaching the entrance to Barry Harbour in the early 1900s.*

Bonnie Doon *at Minehead Pier in the early 1900s.*

Brown's tender book states, 'Approximate prices were given to enable Mr Thompson to work out calculations of interest and insurance'. Once again the tenders were to T.R. Thompson and not the Barry Railway and nothing further came of them. At a directors' meeting on 4 July 1900 the rejection of the Steam Vessels Bill was discussed and it was 'resolved to recommend that an independent company, with a capital of £100,000 be formed and registered'. The Barry company was already thinking of ways and means of running steamers without Parliamentary consent.

With the forthcoming opening of the new Minehead Pier scheduled for May 1901, P&A Campbell Ltd were again approached by the Barry company. The possibility of increased business by way of trips between Barry and Minehead encouraged Alec to agree but during the 1901 season passenger figures showed an alarming drop; 15,483 being carried out of Barry that year, nearly 30,000 less than in 1899. Nevertheless, P&A Campbell Ltd ran out of Barry in 1902 with the *Glen Rosa* continuing to take the Weston sailings; the *Albion* being the Ilfracombe steamer until she hurriedly departed for Southampton at the end of the August Bank Holiday week for the Naval Review.

The weather during the 1902 season had been very poor and only 5,700 passengers had been carried out of Barry. Owing to the lack of passengers the Ilfracombe steamer frequently started from Cardiff before calling at Barry and often arrived at the latter port with little room to spare. The Barry directors complained that the steamers were 'not good enough', but Alec replied that they were not going to run their best steamers out of Barry when they could be more profitably employed elsewhere. On 5 December 1902 P&A Campbell Ltd wrote to the Barry company's general manager:

> At a meeting of our directors held on 1st inst. the results of the past season's trading were discussed, and as a very considerable loss had been again incurred by the service from Barry Pier, the board regret that they do not see their way clear to provide a similar service next year on the same lines.

The Barry company were naturally disappointed at having no steamer service in 1903 and made plans to re-introduce their Steam Vessels Bill in the first possible session of Parliament. Their intentions were soon much talked about in Cardiff and elsewhere in the channel. Alec shrewdly realised that the whole power and wealth of the Barry company would be called upon to force the new Bill through Parliament. The matter was discussed at a directors meeting on 23 November 1903 and Alec was authorised to meet Richard Evans, the Barry company's general manager, and ask him if his company would accept a clause in their Bill limiting the proposed service from Barry.

On 14 December Alec gave an account of this meeting. Mr Evans had stated that the Barry Co. were prepared to insert a clause if P&A Campbell Ltd would not oppose the Bill. Mr W.H. Brown, Campbells' solicitor, was authorised to confer with Alec and to undertake that they would not oppose the Bill provided that the Barry Co. would insert the clause suggested by Mr Balfour Brown KC. The Barry Bill was deposited in Parliament on 21 December 1903 and included the following:

4. (1) It shall be lawful for the Company to provide use maintain and work steam vessels for the conveyance of passengers and their luggage perishable merchandise and also such small consignments of other merchandise as are usually carried by steam vessels constructed for and engaged in such passenger traffic as is by this section authorised to ply to and from Barry on the one hand from and to any ports or places on the south side of the Bristol Channel situate or being between Weston-Super-Mare and Ilfracombe both inclusive on the other hand:

And also for summer excursion traffic to ply in the Bristol Channel eastward of a line drawn from Tenby on the north to Lundy Island and from Lundy Island to Hartland Point on the south and westward of a line to be drawn from Barry on the north to Weston-Super-Mare on the south:

And also for summer excursion traffic arising at Barry or brought over the Barry Railway from Barry to Bristol and Barry to Clevedon, both direct and back Provided that the Company shall not carry passengers out of Bristol or Clevedon other than those brought from Barry and that the voyages of such steam vessels shall always commence and ultimately terminate at Barry.

(2) 'Summer excursion traffic' means the conveyance (between the first day of May and the thirty-first day of October in any year) of passengers and their luggage and also such small consignments of merchandise as are usually carried in steam vessels constructed for and engaged in such traffic.

(3) If the powers conferred upon the Company by this section shall not be bona fide exercised by the Company before the expiration of three years from the passing of this Act then such powers shall cease and determine.

It will be seen that by virtue of this clause – the 'infamous' Clause 4 – the Barry company were completely shut out of Cardiff, Penarth and Newport and could not embark passengers at either Bristol or Clevedon.

1904

The Barry Bill came before the Select Committee on 27 April 1904 and, as foreseen by Alec, the promoters brought a formidable array of power to bear, being represented by no less than four King's Counsellors.

Giving evidence in support of the Bill were Sir John Wolfe Barry, the engineer, who stated that the Barry pontoon, the tunnel and rail extension, which had cost £100,000 to build, could not now be used unless the Barry company ran their own steamers.

Mr Cooper, manager of the Glasgow & South Western Railway, had been brought down from Scotland to state that the position of the Barry Railway was analogous to his company.

Among others called were Commander J.G. Ede ex-RN., the Ilfracombe harbourmaster; Mr R.M. Rowe, clerk of the Ilfracombe Urban District Council, who stated that his council had passed a resolution in favour of the Bill: Mr Riddell, chairman of the Lynton Council, who read a resolution in favour of the Bill passed by his council: Mr Ingleton, clerk of the Minehead Council; Mr Stokes, town clerk at Tenby and Mr William Brace, vice president of the South Wales Miners' Federation; in fact anybody and everybody that the Barry company could rake in to give evidence in favour of the Bill.

A number of meetings of the Barry directors took place during July and August 1904 specifically to discuss the Steam Vessels Act. The only definite reference to the running of steamers appears in the minutes for 4 August:

> The discussion of how the company's powers under this Act are to be brought into operation was continued. It was decided to appoint Robert Forrest and T.R. Thompson a committee to proceed to the north with the Co's. officials to enquire what can be done in the way of getting tenders for two boats suitable for this service and that a special meeting should, if necessary, be thereafter called at the solicitor's office to further consider the matter.

[4 EDW. 7.]   *Barry Railway (Steam Vessels)*   [**Ch. ccxxvii.**]
Act, 1904.

CHAPTER ccxxvii.

An Act to authorise the Barry Railway Company to pro- A.D. 1904.
vide and work steam vessels to raise additional capital
and for other purposes.   [15th August 1904.]

WHEREAS the Barry Railway Company (in this Act called "the Company") have constructed large docks and works at Barry in the county of Glamorgan with special accommodation for the landing and embarking of passengers at all states of the tide and for large vessels and facilities for the shipment and discharge of goods and minerals and with railways connecting their said dock works with the Great Western and other railways in communication with all parts of Great Britain and have expended thereon since the year one thousand eight hundred and eighty-four a sum of five million pounds or thereabouts:

And whereas it would conduce to the public convenience and is expedient that the Company should have powers to provide steam vessels in order to facilitate the transmission of traffic from their railways to ports and places in the Bristol Channel:

And whereas the Company require additional capital for the purposes of this Act and in connection with their authorised undertaking and it is expedient that powers should be conferred upon them to raise additional capital as hereinafter provided and that such further powers should be conferred upon the Company as are hereinafter mentioned:

And whereas the purposes of this Act cannot be effected without the authority of Parliament:

May it therefore please Your Majesty that it may be enacted and be it enacted by the King's most Excellent Majesty by and with the advice and consent of the Lords Spiritual and Temporal

[*Price 6d.*]   A   1

The front page of the Barry Railway (Steam vessels) Act, 1904.

The Barry Railway Steam Vessels Bill was passed, and received Royal Assent on 15 August 1904. At the next directors' meeting, on 19 August, Mr Thompson explained that he and Mr Forrest had been to Glasgow and that a variety of tenders had been received from John Brown & Co. Ltd. It should be noted that the tenders, dated 16 August 1904, were to the Barry Railway and not to Mr Thompson and were itemised as follows:

Tender No 1 – Two paddle steamers, 240ft. by 28ft. 6ins. by 9ft. 9ins., with a guaranteed speed of 19.5 knots. £29,020 each.

Tender No 2 – Two paddle steamers, duplicates of the Juno, with a guaranteed speed of 19.5 knots. £29,790 each.

Tender No 3 – Two paddle steamers, 250ft. by 29ft. by 10ft. 3ins., with five Navy type boilers, with a guaranteed speed of 19.5 knots. £32,320 each.

Tender No 4 – A turbine steamer, 240ft. by 28ft. 6ins. by 9ft. 9ins. with a guaranteed speed of 20 knots. £31,440.

The plans, which had been received with the tenders, were carefully examined and after discussion Lord Windsor moved that the recommendations of the committee, (i.e. Forrest and Thompson), as to the type of vessel should be adopted. It was resolved that the tender for the building of one or two steamers of the second type offered should be accepted; that the committee should endeavour to obtain a reduction in price for two steamers, with full power to contract definitely for one or two steamers on the best possible terms, and that the committee should obtain specifications of the hull, machinery etc. and revise them with the assistance of Capt. Williamson, Superintendent of the Glasgow & South Western Railway steamers.

It should be noted that although John Brown's Tender No.2 stated 'duplicates of the *Juno*' and was so noted in their tender book, this statement refers only to the length, breadth and depth of their hulls – 245ft by 29ft by 9ft 7in. The plans of the Barry Railway ships, Yard Nos 368 and 369, and of the *Juno*, Yard No.331, are still in existence and a comparison shows that the lines of the Barry steamers were to be sharper than those of the *Juno*.

On 3 September 1904 the agreement was signed and sealed with John Brown & Co. Ltd for the construction of the two vessels, the first to cost £29,970 and the second £29,000.

Messrs Forrest and Thompson were appointed to consider the best scheme for the provisional working of the steamers under the terms of the 1904 Act. The minutes of the directors' meeting of 28 October 1904 stated:

Steam Vessels. This question was reported on by the committee dealing therewith and their action was approved.

One cannot be but curious as to why the minutes of the Barry company were so guarded and obscure; the answer being that plans were already being laid to circumvent the restrictions embodied in Clause 4 of the Act.

As may well be imagined, all sorts of rumours were rife concerning the new Barry steamers, particularly in respect of their speed. One 'flight of fancy' credited them with a speed in excess of 21 knots! Another rumour anticipated that the Barry steamers were going to run P&A Campbell Ltd 'out of the channel'.

Early in 1904 the newspapers reported on the rebuilding of Birnbeck Pier. On 25 January the *Western Mail* stated:

> Great activity is being manifested in the Weston Super Mare pier undertaking. The old landing jetty at Birnbeck Pier, which was almost entirely demolished by the great September gale, is being replaced by a structure of steel, wider and larger than the old wooden jetty, and the work promises to be completed before Easter, (early April), so that the daily boat service between Cardiff and Weston may be expected to commence at the usual time. Five spans of this bridge are already up and the head of the old jetty, which was left standing almost intact after the gale, is now being removed; piles and joists being substituted.

Completion of the work was slightly delayed but on the evening of 3 May 1904 the *Waverley*, dressed overall and carrying a full complement of passengers from Cardiff, performed the reopening ceremony.

The White Funnel Fleet's 1904 season passed uneventfully in both channels, although the Directors' Report stated that 'The results of the trading on the South Coast show a considerable increase'.

Alec reported to his directors on 7 November 1904 that an order for new paddle wheels for the *Westward Ho* had been placed with Barclay & Curle at a cost of £1,359 and added that tenders had been requested from several Clyde shipyards for the building of a new steamer. A special meeting was called for 25 November, the minutes of which state:

> Capt. Campbell explained that the meeting had been called to consider a quotation from Messrs. Hutson of £15,500 for a new steamer. Several other firms had been asked to quote but had declined on the grounds that with the work they already had on hand they would be unable to give delivery in May next, the time asked for...
>
> Capt. Campbell pointed out that the quote of £15,500 was very low but that unless the *Bonnie Doon* or one of the other steamers could be disposed of, there would be difficulty in finding the necessary funds for the purchase of the new steamer. After some discussion the Secretary was instructed to apply to the bank for an advance of £8,200 on a first mortgage.

On 30 November the secretary reported that the bank considered the application premature and were not disposed to finance any part of the building of a new

Albion *in the river Usk in the early 1900s.*

Westward Ho *passing an inward bound cargo ship in the river Avon in the early 1900s.*

Britannia *arriving at Bristol in the early 1900s.*

Westward Ho *leaving Cardiff in the early 1900s.*

Above and Opposite: *Ilfracombe in 1904. The light cruiser HMS* Spartan *lay at anchor offshore between 22 and 25 August, during which time one of her guns was taken ashore in readiness for a programme of sporting events in Hillsborough Park. Field gun drill and a number of competitions took place which included a tug of war between the stokers and donkey races for the officers. These photographs show the gun being taken back to the warship. The* Cambria *and* Albion *are berthed at the Stone Bench.*

steamer. It appeared that the bank also thought that the Barry steamers were going to put the White Funnel steamers out of business.

On the same date Alec stated that the company who ran the *Alexandra* from Hastings during the 1903 season were anxious to obtain another steamer. They had been offered the *Bonnie Doon* but did not bite. Another blow fell in December 1904 when the Law Guarantee Society stated that they would be prepared to advance only a partial mortgage. The matter was left to Alec to deal with as he thought fit but by the end of the year he reported that it was now too late to place an order for a new steamer for delivery by the following summer. The matter was discussed by the board and it was decided to postpone the order until August 1905.

Little of interest appeared in the Barry minute books until 10 February 1905, when something of a 'bombshell' was dropped:

> Mr Thompson proposed the following resolution which was unanimously agreed to
> – 'It was resolved that the arrangement made with Messrs. Symonds, Lewis, Radford
> and Jones for the sale to them of the steamboats now in the course of construction by
> Messrs. John Brown & Co. of Glasgow, and for the provision of a service in accordance
> with the Co.'s. Act of Parliament be confirmed and that the seal of the Co. be affixed
> thereto.' It was also resolved that notice be given that this last resolution be brought for
> confirmation at the next board meeting.

There was absolutely nothing in the minute books referring to any proposed arrangement, nor was there any resolution proposing a sale, nor any reference to a sale. The whole matter was a devious and discreditable act by the Barry Railway to avoid the restrictions of the 1904 Act.

THE BARRY STEAMSHIPS

1905

The first of the two steamers ordered by the Barry Railway was launched at John Brown's Clydebank yard on 24 February 1905 and christened *Gwalia* by the wife of Robert Forrest, one of the Barry company directors and also one of the promoters of the company in 1883.

The Barry company's minute book bears two obscure entries for the board meeting of 3 March 1905, the first of which stated:

> Steamboats. The resolution passed was confirmed.

This referred to T.R. Thompson's proposal that the two new steamers should be 'sold' to the syndicate of Symonds, Lewis, Radford and Jones.

The second entry stated:

> Bankers. It was resolved that the Seal of the Company be affixed to the security required by the bankers, a draft of which was produced.

It appears that the bankers were somewhat apprehensive of future events regarding the syndicate and were safeguarding themselves. The same could be said of John Brown & Co. who wrote to the Barry company requesting that authority under the Seal of the Barry Railway should be given in order for them to make out the builder's certificates in the names of the four owners of the new steamers.

The first press report of the syndicate appeared in the financial column of the *Western Mail* of 7 March 1905:

> It is authoritatively stated that the two passenger steamboats for the Barry Railway Co. for the channel service have been acquired by a syndicate consisting of four local gentlemen, and that the vessels will begin running in May. The market had never regarded the establishment of such a service under the direct auspices of the Barry

The launch of the Gwalia *at John Brown's yard, Clydebank, on 24 February 1905.*
(National Archives of Scotland. Ref UCS1/368/7)

The Gwalia *fitting out at John Brown's yard during March 1905. (National Archives of Scotland. Ref*
UCS1/119/368/1)

Above and below: *The Gwalia fitting out at John Brown's yard during March 1905. (National Archives of Scotland. Ref UCS1/118/368/4 and UCS1/118/368)*

Co. as being likely to prove a great additional source of income, and the action of the directors in transferring the new steamers to a syndicate has thus met with more or less general approval. The company, however, will still profit from any increase in its passenger traffic which may follow the operation of a direct service between Barry and the holiday resorts on the other side of the channel.

The members of the syndicate were:

William Thomas Symonds. Manager. A timber importer, coal exporter and owner of two small tramp steamers. A shareholder in the Barry Railway Company.

William North Lewis. Managing partner of Insole's who were among the founders of the Barry Railway Company and major shareholders.

Howard Edmund Radford. A son-in-law of T. R. Thompson, married to one of Thompson's four daughters.

Herbert Rees Jones (Junior). Son of the late Herbert Rees Jones of the Ocean Collieries; director of the Barry Railway Company and one of its founders.

A cheque was supposed to have passed from the syndicate to the Barry company for the purchase of the two steamers; this cheque being drawn on an overdraft at the City branch of the Metropolitan Bank in Birmingham, the overdraft having been guaranteed by the Barry Railway.

There was no trace of a Bill of Sale to the syndicate by the Barry Railway and as we shall later discover, there never was any sale. It was T.R. Thompson's ploy to run the steamers outside the provisions of the 1904 Act by claiming that they now belonged to a private company – 'The Barry & Bristol Channel Steamship Company' – but there never was such a company; it was merely an alias for the Barry Railway.

The *Gwalia* ran her preliminary trials on 20 March 1905 and went up-river next day to Govan for bottom scraping and painting. She returned to Clydebank on 22 March, the day on which her sister ship was launched and christened *Devonia* by Mrs Howard Edmund Radford, one of T.R. Thompson's daughters.

At 09.40 on 23 March the *Gwalia* sailed for her official trials on the Skelmorlie measured mile. Her highest speed on one run was 20.57 knots and her best mean speed 19.81 knots, exceeding the guaranteed speed by almost a third of a knot. It must be pointed out, however, that her official trials were run 'light', with the minimum of coal and water and the least possible deadweight aboard. Comparing the preliminary and official trials one finds that on the latter the mean displacement was 17 tons less than on the former and her mean draught was only 6ft 3in. These trial speeds were never to be repeated in service when loaded with passengers, full bunkers and full fresh water tanks.

The two Barry steamers were undoubtedly most handsome vessels with their well raked large diameter funnels, and massive paddles and paddle boxes. Their paddle wheels were 14ft 11in in diameter over the axis of the float pins and their seven

Gwalia *on preliminary trials in the Firth of Clyde, 20 March 1905.*

Gwalia *on official trials in the Firth of Clyde. 23 March 1905.*

paddle floats measured 12ft 9in by 3ft 9in depth. Compound diagonal engines had cylinders 34.5in by 71in in diameter with a 60in stroke. The boilers were 18ft 11in long by 16ft 8in of the double ended return type with eight furnaces working under forced draught at 150lb per square inch; coal consumption was correspondingly high at about 2½ tons per hour at full speed.

Their funnels were buff with narrow black tops; the saloon strakes white and the hulls black with red boot topping. Their deckhouses were of varnished teak and the ventilators were silverine. A most ornate paddle box design was picked out in gold on white, with the Barry dragon in gold on a red circle surrounded with a scroll bearing the legend 'Barry Steamships 1905'; the whole supported by two unicorns 'passant'.

As in the *Brighton Queen* access to the main deck was well covered, with companionways to the main deck under the bridge and the after deckhouse. The latter had a ladder at its after end and a deep, canvas dodger – very comfortable for those who wished to pay the extra 6d for sitting aloft.

The forward saloon ports were small and rectangular but the after saloon had large square windows. The sponsons were typical Clydebank design with the straight run from the paddle boxes to the ships' sides and were unusually high from the water line.

Below decks the accommodation was superb. In contrast to Campbells' myrtle Utrecht Velvet the main saloons were upholstered in bright blue plush. A Ladies Tea Room; Gentlemens' Smoke Room upholstered in green morocco leather; a fruit and sweet stall, together with a fine dining saloon, completed the ensemble.

The engine rooms were not cased in Campbell fashion but were left open – Clyde style – with rails around with wide teak tops. The engine room ventilators on the reserved deck were originally very low, the cowls barely reaching the top level of the canvas dodger, thus scooping little air and making the engine room unbearably hot. Towards the end of the 1905 season these ventilators were raised by 2ft, the *Devonia* being the first so treated. Before 1906, however, they were raised a further 3ft.

It was peculiar that the lifeboats and lifebuoys had at first 'Barry' as the port of registry for the ships were never registered there. Although there was a Custom House at Barry there was no register, the ships being registered at Cardiff. Later in the season 'Cardiff' replaced 'Barry' on the boats and lifebuoys.

On 29 March 1905 the *Gwalia* left Clydebank for Greenock where she was formally accepted by her owners, who were still noted in John Brown's records as 'The Barry Railway Company'. Capt. James W. James was her master; formerly with Campbells he had been 'waged and won' by the offer of a greatly increased salary.

The *Gwalia* did not leave Greenock until 09.30 on 11 April 1905 and entered the Barry Dock Basin at 10.00 on the following day, having averaged 16 knots on the passage south. A large crowd had assembled to greet her arrival and gave her a rousing welcome, eulogistic descriptions being given in the Barry and Cardiff newspapers.

She made her maiden trip, to Ilfracombe, on Wednesday 19 April 1905; it was not, however, a public trip. The Barry directors, the syndicate, and invited guests, numbering about 140 in total, were aboard when she left Cardiff at 09.30 for Penarth,

Gwalia arriving at Ilfracombe on what is believed to be her maiden trip with the Barry Railway directors, the syndicate and invited guests aboard, Wednesday 19 April 1905.

Barry and Ilfracombe. There she embarked further guests and a short cruise was made around Woolacombe Bay. Two sittings were held for the six-course luncheon and in reply to a speech at the second sitting Mr Herbert Rees Jones flamboyantly remarked, 'It would rest with the travelling public whether the company put down half-a-dozen more boats this season'. It is assumed that he meant the Barry Railway for the Barry & Bristol Channel Steamship Co. had no capital and no shares!

Next day the *Western Mail* gave the *Gwalia* a good write-up. The article began:

TRIAL TRIP OF THE STEAMSHIP GWALIA.
NEW COMPANY'S PROMISING START.
The Barry and Bristol Channel Steamship Company have made a very auspicious start to their first season...

and continued with an account of the trip as detailed above.

The *Gwalia's* first public sailings took place on Maundy Thursday 20 April. The advertised times were as follows:

Dep. Cardiff 07.30 for Penarth and Weston. Dep. Weston 08.15 for Cardiff.
Dep. Cardiff 09.20 for Penarth and Ilfracombe.
Dep. Ilfracombe 16.20 for Penarth and Cardiff.
Dep. Cardiff 19.30 for Penarth and Weston. Dep. Weston 20.30 for Cardiff.

On the same day as the *Gwalia* began sailing – Maundy Thursday 20 April – the *Cambria* made her first trip of the season, to Ilfracombe. On the return journey she left Ilfracombe at 15.40, called off Lynmouth and arrived at Penarth Pier at 17.37. The *Western Mail*, obviously forgetting that a strong spring flood tide was running at the time, claimed that on this return trip 'A speed of 22 knots was maintained'. (Perhaps the *Cambria* was travelling, on times, at a speed approaching 22 knots, especially in the upper reaches of the channel, but this would have been 'over the ground'. As fast as she was, the *Cambria's* speed 'through the water' would have been a few knots less).

This item was copied by the Ilfracombe newspapers and sparked off a considerable controversy. An angry letter was written to the *Chronicle* by Mr William Jones, the Barry company's Ilfracombe agent, who offered £5 to anyone who could prove that the *Cambria* had sustained 22 knots! The ensuing correspondence contained many fanciful claims and counter-claims but, needless to say, no factual evidence was forthcoming.

The *Devonia* ran her preliminary trials, most unusually, on Good Friday 21 April 1905. She followed the same routine as the *Gwalia* in going up river to the Govan Graving Dock for bottom cleaning and painting before returning to Clydebank and running official trials on 29 April. Her best speed was 20.11 knots and her best mean speed 19.74 knots. She left Clydebank for Cardiff, direct, on the morning of 2 May, under the command of Capt. John Henry Denman, another former Campbell master, and arrived at Cardiff on the following morning. It was not until 11 May 1905 that she ran her maiden trip, to Ilfracombe.

The Cardiff newspapers *Western Mail* and *South Wales Daily News* were owned by the Duncan family who were large shareholders in the Barry Railway. Not surprisingly the proprietors lost no opportunity in running articles lauding the Barry steamers, and accounts of races and a variety of other incidents are unquestionably biased. As an example the *South Wales Daily News* published an article on 11 May 1905 headlined 'Bristol Channel Passenger Service – Exciting Race', describing how the *Gwalia* and *Cambria* left Ilfracombe on the previous day and engaged each other in a race to Barry Pier. The reporter appeared to be acting on the age old maxim of some journalists – 'Never let the truth interfere with a good story'! To begin with he seemed to be quite unaware that the *Cambria* was not calling at Barry Pier.

The article detailed how the two steamers left the pier at the same time but added that the *Cambria* got under way first – 'because she was shorter' – whatever that may mean?! The *Cambria* reached Lynmouth first, had shipped her passengers and proceeded while the *Gwalia* was embarking hers. It was then stated that the *Gwalia* overhauled the *Cambria* and arrived at Barry Pier 150 yards ahead.

This drew a most indignant letter from Mr W.H. Guy, Campbells' Cardiff agent, who wrote to the *South Wales Daily News*:

I notice in your Thursday issue a report of an 'Interesting Race' between the passenger steamers *Cambria* and *Gwalia*. As the facts there stated are not true, I would thank you to correct same in your next issue. It is quite correct that the *Cambria* and *Gwalia* left Ilfracombe together and arrived at Lynmouth in the same order, but after leaving

Gwalia *leaving Cardiff, April/May 1905.*

Gwalia *arriving at Ilfracombe, April/May 1905.*

Above and below. Gwalia *leaving Ilfracombe, April/May 1905.*

Devonia *on preliminary trials in the Firth of Clyde, Good Friday 21 April 1905.*

Devonia *on official trials in the Firth of Clyde, Saturday 29 April 1905.*

Ilfracombe from Hillsborough in May 1905, with Devonia *at the Stone Bench.*

Dining saloon of the Gwalia.

Lynmouth the *Cambria* came direct to Penarth and Cardiff and did not touch Barry Pier, and it is not correct to say that the *Gwalia* passed the *Cambria* and arrived at Barry Pier 150 yards ahead. As a matter of fact the *Cambria* arrived <u>off</u> Barry some 500 yards (or thereabouts) ahead of the *Gwalia*. Furthermore, no arrangements were made to test the speeds of these steamers and on the part of the *Cambria* there was no racing, and it is the intention of my company to do no racing, but to do what we have always done, our journeys as expeditiously as possible consistent with the comfort and safety of our passengers.

Both the *Gwalia* and *Devonia* were taken out of service at intervals during May 1905. The *Western Mail* reported on 17 May:

> The steamship *Gwalia*, of the Barry Steamship Co., is undergoing re-painting which will completely change her external appearance. The funnels, hitherto yellow, will be red with a deep, black band at the top, and the hull will be a light slate colour. The *Devonia* will be similarly treated.

The reason for the change of colour scheme is unknown but most people agreed that the change was for the better; the light grey hulls, in contrast with the rich, cherry red funnels gave the ships an even more striking appearance. As might have been expected they now became known as 'The Red Funnel Line'.

Before the full season's sailings commenced at Whitsun adverts began to appear daily in the Cardiff newspapers:

> BARRY RAILWAY & BARRY & BRISTOL CHANNEL STEAMSHIP CO.
> Daily Service Between Cardiff, Lynmouth and Ilfracombe.
> An Express Boat Train (without stop) leaves Cardiff Riverside Station Daily at 9.35am and runs Direct to Barry Pier to meet the Steamer for Ilfracombe.
> EXPRESS TRAINS AND FAST STEAMERS.

When the tide was suitable the steamer left Cardiff Pier Head at 09.35, Penarth 09.45 and Barry at 10.10. When the tide did not serve the steamer sailed from Barry Pier only at 10.10. A train awaited the return of the steamer in the evening even if she was continuing to Penarth and Cardiff. This daily arrangement, during which the Riverside porters announced 'Ilfracombe Boat Express', was to continue for many years.

The *South Wales Daily News* of Monday 29 May 1905 reported on the 'splendidly successful' afternoon excursion of the *Gwalia* to Ilfracombe on the previous Saturday:

> ...When the *Gwalia* left Cardiff at half past two she had her full complement of passengers and the company regret that their boat was unable to call at Penarth to take on board many other people who were waiting on the pier.

Gwalia *and* Normandy *at Ilfracombe in 1905.*

Gwalia *in the river Avon in 1905.*

Devonia *arriving at Weston in 1905.*

Gwalia *leaving Barry in 1905.*

The *Gwalia* made a very quick passage and it is claimed that her time from the moment she swung clear at Cardiff to the throwing of the first rope ashore at Ilfracombe, 1 hour and 57 minutes, beats all previous records by many minutes. We understand that the company are more than pleased with the public patronage bestowed upon their boats up to the present.

Unfortunately this is another example of inaccurate reporting. Both the *Gwalia* and *Cambria* sailed from Cardiff at 14.30 that afternoon for Penarth and Ilfracombe. From several fragments of surviving information it is apparent that the *Cambria* called at Penarth Pier but the *Gwalia,* which was not full, did not call in order to get ahead of the *Cambria*. Which of the steamers arrived at Ilfracombe first is not recorded but the *Gwalia's* time of one hour fifty-seven minutes was by no means a record; the *Cambria* and *Britannia* frequently made the passage between Cardiff and Ilfracombe in under two hours with, of course, the help of fast tides.

Regrettably, hardly any detailed accounts of the racing between the Red and White Funnel steamers have survived. The P&A Campbell records for the period were destroyed many years ago, as were the Ilfracombe Pier records when a heavy gale tore the roof off the hut on the pier in which they were stored, allowing the rain to turn them into a sodden mass. Nevertheless sufficient fragments remain to indicate that the *Britannia* and *Cambria* usually had the advantage over the *Devonia* and *Gwalia*. This is not to suggest that the two former ships won every time, but the Red Funnel Line had no masters to equal Peter Campbell, Dan Taylor and Allan Livingstone. These men had been brought up in Clyde racing circles and knew all the tricks and dodges, and had quickly adapted themselves to the vagaries of the Bristol Channel. For instance, when racing from Lynmouth to Ilfracombe against a flood tide it was essential to gain the 'inside berth'; that is a course near the land where the force of the incoming tide was less. However, care had to be taken not to allow the other vessel to press the inner one too closely to the shore for at Highveer Point, Heddonsmouth, the inner ship would become embayed. She would then have to slow down or stop in order to move out sufficiently to clear the point.

Many years ago an old Ilfracombe resident described a typical day on the pier in those halcyon days:

Imagine Ilfracombe Pier one fine sunny, summer's day in 1905 or 1906. The *Brighton* and *Normandy* have arrived earlier from Swansea, have embarked their passengers and departed for other destinations. The time is ten minutes to one-o-clock and a large crowd has gathered on the pier, many of them holiday-makers, some residents, but all of whom are going to be late for lunch.

Fred Birmingham, Campbells' agent, wearing his customary straw boater, has just arrived bringing the news that the Lynmouth agent has telephoned to say that the *Gwalia* and *Britannia* have embarked their passengers and have left Lynmouth level with each other. The news spreads through the crowd like a forest fire, and bets are being freely offered and taken as to the winner, for some of the crowd are Barry partisans and others support Campbells.

The minutes tick by. Those 'in the know' have seated themselves on the concrete wall on the north of the pier, their eyes glued to the gap in the green-capped rocks of Rillage Point. Two, three or more minutes pass and then a cloud of smoke appears behind the point and to the cheers of the Barry supporters the red and black funnels of the *Gwalia* glide into sight. A couple of seconds later the white funnel of the *Britannia* appears, and she has the inside berth!

Around Rillage Point they come, Capt. Peter almost shaving the rocks, but he knows exactly how much water he has underneath him and the *Britannia* tears through the water towards Beacon Point, Hillsborough. It can be seen now that the *Gwalia* is dropping astern.

The flags go up on the pier; the letter W for the *Britannia*, which means she is to take the Stone Bench, and the letter K for the *Gwalia*, denoting the face of the pier. The *Britannia* is rapidly drawing away now and must be two lengths ahead of the *Gwalia*, but Capt. Peter keeps her going at full speed and does not ring down for 'Half' until he is opposite Raparree Cove, then 'Stop', then 'Full astern', and the *Britannia* glides alongside her berth with the utmost precision, her sponson knuckle gently nudges the wooden piles and the heaving lines are thrown ashore. The *Britannia* has beaten the *Gwalia* by a minute and a half!

And so it went on, day after day...

T.R. Thompson had reported to his directors on 5 May 1905 that the company had the offer of an additional steamer which they were 'desirous of purchasing subject to their agreement with the Barry Railway Co. being extended so as to apply to this steamer'. In other words the Barry Railway was being asked to put up the money for another vessel.

On 29 May 1905 the *Western Mail* reported:

> The Barry Passenger Steamer Syndicate have just acquired the North Wales passenger steamship Rhos Colwyn and have re-named her *Westonia* for the Cardiff to Weston service. The vessel is now in Dublin undergoing repairs and is expected at Barry...next week...

The *Rhos Colwyn*, ex-*Sussex Belle*, ex-*Tantallon Castle* was sold for £12,960, not to the Barry & Bristol Channel Steamship Co. but to a Cardiff merchant, Charles Edward Evans, another son-in-law of T.R. Thompson and a large shareholder in the Barry Railway. The ship was registered at Cardiff on 10 June 1905, Evans being her registered owner but W.J. Symonds was registered as her manager.

The actual Bill of Sale to Evans, (it was the Barry Railway who paid for her), was dated 9 June 1905 but by mid-May the ship had already been placed in the hands of the Dublin Dockyard Co. for repairs and repainting. The *Westonia* ran trials in Dublin Bay on 7 June and was stated by the Barry and Cardiff newspapers to have

Gwalia *leaving Newport in 1905.*

Britannia *outward bound in the river Usk on 6 July 1905.*

Westward Ho *leaving Sharpness in the 1900s.*

With steam to spare, the Westward Ho *leaves Ilfracombe on a charter trip in 1905.*

Ravenswood *off Penarth in 1905.*

Albion *in the river Avon in the 1900s.*

Left to right: Gwalia, Cambria *and* Albion *at Ilfracombe in 1905.*

achieved a speed of 18 knots but this must be regarded as an exaggeration. She left Dublin after completing her trials and arrived in Barry on the following morning, her first trip being from Cardiff to Weston on 10 June 1905.

The *Gwalia* made her first trip to Bristol on Thursday 1 June 1905, running a return trip from Cardiff. This destination was quite in order; Clause 4 of the Barry Railway (Steam Vessels) Act allowed them to land passengers at Bristol but not to embark fresh passengers. However, the next day's adverts appeared in the newspapers advertising the *Gwalia* for a return trip on Monday 5 June from Bristol to Clevedon, Cardiff, Penarth, Lynmouth and Ilfracombe, also a single trip that evening to Cardiff. A succession of trips from Bristol was also advertised for the following week, short ones as the tides were not suitable, but from 20 June the Ilfracombe trips recommenced.

It must not be supposed that Campbells were doing nothing to combat the Barry Railway. Alec had explained to his directors at the beginning of April 1905 the attitude adopted by the Barry Railway in the proposed running of their steamers. After some discussion it was decided to leave the matter with Alec and the director, Mr Alfred Deeds, to take Counsel's opinion should they consider it advisable – they did!

The Barry Railway minutes for 2 June 1905 record:

Barry & Bristol Channel Co. The correspondence with Mr H.W. Bliss, (Campbells' London solicitor), was taken as read. It was resolved that the secretary inform him that his clients are under a misapprehension, and that the solicitor be instructed to take all the necessary steps to protect the Barry Railway Co's interests, and also that Messrs. Forrest and Thompson be a committee to deal with the matter.

Westonia *leaving Cardiff in 1905.*

Westonia *at Bristol in 1905.*

Each member of the syndicate – Symonds, North Lewis, Rees Jones and Radford – had already sworn affidavits to the effect that they were the legal owners of the steamers. In the light of subsequent events they were extremely lucky not to be charged with perjury.

The Barry Railway's solicitor told his directors, on 28 July, that he had been served with a Writ of Summons and a Notice of Motion by Mr H. W. Bliss, Capt. Alec's London solicitor. The motion came up on 8 August 1905 in the Chancery Division before Mr Justice Swinfen-Eady, but owing to the affidavits sworn by the syndicate it was not proceeded with. On 16 June 1905 adverts had appeared in the Cardiff newspapers:

RED FUNNEL LINE
REDUCTION IN FARES
The Barry & Bristol Channel Steamship Co. beg to give notice that on and after 17 June the fares from Cardiff to the various places in the channel served by their steamers, THE RED FUNNEL LINE, will be as follows – Cardiff to Weston 1/- single, 1/6 return; Bristol 1/6 single, 2/- return; Lynmouth and Ilfracombe single (foredeck) 2/6, return (foredeck) 3/-. Single (saloon) 3/6, return (saloon) 4/-.

P&A Campbell Ltd had to follow suit, their advert appearing on 17 June. Naturally these low fares simply did not pay but the Barry company thought that with their great railway revenue that they could afford to 'starve out' Campbells and take over the whole of the Bristol Channel steamer traffic.

While all this activity proceeded between the channel's main protagonists, the *Brighton* and *Normandy* continued their services from Swansea with little incident until Friday 14 July. The *Brighton* had sailed from Swansea at 08.00 bound for

Brighton *aground on the Cherrystones, Mumbles, Friday 14 July 1905.*

Normandy *arriving at Ilfracombe in the mid-1900s.*

Mumbles and Ilfracombe. A dense fog enveloped her as she crossed Swansea Bay and although her speed was reduced to dead slow she ran aground on the Cherrystones, a reef to the south-east of Mumbles Head. Fortunately, as the tide ebbed she was found to be well supported for the whole of her length and she floated off without difficulty shortly before 13.00. She entered the Prince of Wales Dry Dock at Swansea having sustained damage to several bow plates but was back in service after about a week.

Both of the Swansea steamers encountered a small measure of competition, not only from each other but from the Red Funnel ships which had started calling at Mumbles Pier on their way to Tenby; the *Gwalia* having made the first such trip on 5 July 1905. On Wednesday 19 July, however, adverts appeared in the Swansea newspapers for a trip on the following day to Ilfracombe and Clovelly, leaving Pockett's Wharf at 09.00. It is a possibility that the *Brighton's* owners had invited the Red Funnel steamers to call in order to keep business away from the *Normandy*. Pockett's held a long lease on their wharf from the Swansea Harbour Trust but the latter had no intention of allowing the Barry Railway to even get a toe in the water at Swansea. The Trust ruled that while the lease allowed the Pockett steamers to use the wharf without further charge, any other company must pay a charge of £5 every time their ship touched the quay wall. Even the Barry company with its enormous wealth were not willing to pay £10 for a day trip or £20 for two half-day trips so all further trips that season were run from Mumbles Pier.

Swansea was not the only port in which the Barry steamers tried to become established. They ran a number of trips from Newport, the first of which, by the *Gwalia* on 15 July, was a charter to Minehead, to take the 4th Battalion, South Wales Borderers to their summer camp. She performed another charter on 20 July, this time from Port Talbot to Ilfracombe for the annual outing of the Aberavon and Port Talbot shop assistants.

The weather during the summer of 1905 was predominantly good, but 'Boisterous Channel Trips' on 8 September were reported by the *Western Mail*:

> ...a strong south westerly gale prevailed in the Bristol Channel, and the advertised trips of the *Devonia* and *Cambria* proved the most tempestuous of the season... The passage down channel was made against a stiff breeze until Nash Point was reached, and from there to the Mumbles the vessels had to fight their way in the teeth of a gale which was every moment increasing in force, and against seas which constantly swept the decks, causing most of the passengers to seek dryer and more comfortable quarters in the saloons. At Mumbles most of the passengers landed, but the steamers continued their journeys towards Tenby. When off Port Eynon, however, the force of the gale was so terrific that it was decided to return to Mumbles, and as the storm showed no sign of abating, a large number of the passengers decided to return to Cardiff by train. The *Devonia* left Mumbles at 6.30pm and the *Cambria* followed an hour later with only 70 or 80 passengers aboard. Both wind and sea were then with the steamers but the seas were so high that all the saloon shutters were closed, and to keep clear of the coast, the steamers made a great circuit, the *Cambria* even rounding the Scarweather. Between Mumbles and the lightship the severity of the gale was greater than any experienced since the destructive one of two years ago. The decks were constantly swept with spray and movement on deck was impossible...Both steamers, however, returned safely, the *Devonia* arriving at Barry shortly after 9pm and the *Cambria* reaching Cardiff at 10.45pm.

The three Red Funnel steamers enjoyed a relatively trouble free season in 1905. The *Devonia*, however, broke down off Rhoose on her way from Barry to Mumbles on 16 September. The exact nature of the breakdown has not been ascertained but was serious enough for the *Gwalia*, also making her way down channel, to be sent for and to take off her passengers. The *Devonia* was towed back to Barry by two tugs and was reported to have been back in service on the following day.

The White Funnel steamers also experienced a good season. Apart from the ongoing 'skulduggery' of the Barry Railway, little of great interest took place behind the scenes. Alec reported to the directors in September 1905 that the *Albion* had been inspected by representatives of the Hamburg–Amerika Line and that if they should decide to buy her he would recommend that the board should dispose of her and to place an order for a new steamer. The Hamburg–Amerika Line, however, decided against her purchase.

Two totally erroneous newspaper articles had appeared during the course of the season. The first, in the *Ilfracombe Gazette* of 7 July 1905, stated:

THREE NEW BOATS FOR MESSRS. CAMPBELL
...We understand that Messrs. P.&A Campbell Ltd have given orders for three steamers to be built on the Clyde during the winter...each vessel will steam at 23 knots.

Devonia *arriving at Ilfracombe, 1905.*

The second was even more extraordinary and appeared in the Cardiff newspapers on 18 September:

TURBINE STEAMER FOR P. & A. CAMPBELL LTD.
TO BE READY FOR NEXT SEASON.

Messrs. P. & A. Campbell Ltd. of Bristol have just ordered a turbine steamer from Messrs. Denny Bros., Dumbarton. The new steamer, which is to be ready for next season's service, will have accommodation for 2000 passengers, and is practically a replica of the *Queen Alexandra*, whose steaming on the Clyde was responsible for much of the early success of the new type of engine. She will therefore be 270ft. in length, 32ft. in breadth, 11ft. deep and of 800 tons gross. Her specified sea speed is to be 20 knots but it is likely, in accordance with precedent, that this will work out at over 21 knots. Her manoeuvring qualities are guaranteed by the fact that on trials she must show ability to stop dead in her own length when going at 12 knots. The price is said to be £40,000.

Where this absurd yarn originated is a complete mystery. It has even been asserted that not only did P&A Campbell Ltd place an order for the steamer, but that during the course of building she was turned over to the General Steam Navigation Co. of London and completed as the *Kingfisher*. Neither of these wild assumptions has any basis in fact. In Denny's records the letter of enquiry from the GSN still exists; so does Denny's reply and their tender. There is, in Denny's records, no correspondence whatsoever with P&A Campbell Ltd. Neither is there anything in the Campbell minute books relating to such a steamer, so the whole story must be regarded as a complete fabrication. However, a meeting of Campbell directors was called for on 9 October 1905 to consider a quotation from Hutson's for 'an improved *Britannia*', not at the low

Gwalia *at Ilfracombe in 1905.*

Gwalia *heading westward from Ilfracombe in 1905.*

Ilfracombe in 1905. Offshore, either the Gwalia *or* Devonia *passes, while the tops of her sister's funnels are just visible at the face of the pier. The other vessels,* (from left to right), *are* Bonnie Doon, Cambria, Brighton, Albion *and* Britannia.

figure of £15,500 quoted by them in 1904 but at the new price of £22,500. The order had to be placed by 13 October 1905 to ensure delivery for 1906. The board adjourned until 11 October when it was stated that £18,000 would be the maximum sum that could be raised by mortgage. The matter was left to Alec to place or abandon the order as he thought best. The order was abandoned, Alec being well aware that the *Britannia* and *Cambria* had both proved capable of dealing with the Red Funnel steamers.

The Barry Railway were, however, thinking of new tonnage. Two tenders were submitted to 'The Barry & Bristol Channel Steamship Co., Cardiff' in September 1905. The first was for 'a proposed paddle steamer similar to the *Brighton Queen* but with arrangements as in the *Gwalia* and *Devonia*', at a price of approximately £26,000. The second was for 'a proposed paddle steamer for ferry purposes similar to the Glasgow & South Western Railway's *Mars*', at a price of approximately £20,500. Neither tender was accepted.

The momentous 1905 season ended with both the Red and White funnel steamers finishing the Cardiff to Weston service on 16 October. The officers and crews of the three Red Funnel ships were entertained to dinner at the Marine Hotel, Barry Island. One of the syndicate members, Mr Herbert Rees Jones, in making a speech stated:

> The Red Funnel Line has come to stay, and in the words of the old song 'We've got the ships, we've got the men and we've got the money too'.

He neglected to mention, however, that it was the Barry Railway's money!

Cambria *at the breakwater, Porthcawl, in 1905.*

Britannia *approaches Ilfracombe Pier after lying at anchor offshore in the mid-1900s.*

Glen Rosa *arriving at Eastbourne in the 1900s.*

A composite postcard showing the Glen Rosa *off Cowes in the 1900s.*

AN AFTERNOON AT EASTBOURNE IN THE MID–1900S

The Brighton Queen *departs.*

The Glen Rosa *arrives while the* Brighton Queen *heads towards Brighton.*

Above: *The* Glen Rosa *embarks her passengers.*

Right: *The* Glen Rosa *departs on a channel cruise.*

Above and left: *Aboard* Brighton Queen.

Brighton Queen *arriving at Palace Pier, Brighton, in the 1900s.*

Brighton Queen *at Boulogne in the 1900s.*

LIES AND LITIGATION

1906

On 1 January 1906 two significant developments took place with regard to the Red Funnel steamers. Firstly, Charles Edward Evans sold the *Westonia* to the syndicate – Symonds, North Lewis, Rees Jones and Radford; the Bill of Sale being made out to them on the same day. Secondly, a Deed of Covenant was made between the Barry Railway and the members of the syndicate; this supplemented the agreement of March 1905 in which T.R. Thomson proposed that the *Gwalia* and *Devonia* should be 'sold' to them.

In the new deed the steamers were ostensibly to belong to the syndicate but the Barry Railway was to supply the money for running them. P&A Campbell's legal advisers sought and obtained a legal order of discovery under which the syndicate and the Barry company was forced to disclose the terms of both the 1905 agreement and the Deed of Covenant.

When the Motion came up on 20 April 1906 in the High Court, Chancery Division, again before Mr Justice Swinfen-Eady, counsel for P&A Campbell Ltd requested an interim injunction restraining the Barry Railway and the syndicate from running the steamers *Ultra Vires*, (outside the law), to Clause 4 of the Act of 1904. After hearing the evidence the judge commented that 'The four gentlemen merely lent their names to the railway company for a salary'. He then delivered his judgement:

> Under the circumstances I think it is my duty to interfere by granting an injunction restraining the Barry Railway Company and the remaining defendants from carrying out the provisions of the agreement of 1905, the Deed of Covenant of January 1906, and as regards the Barry Railway Company from applying any of its funds.

The interim injunction was to stand until the actual case came to court in 1907; the delay being due to the great difficulties experienced by P&A Campbell's solicitor in obtaining full disclosure by the defendants of books and papers which he considered essential to the proper trial of the Action.

Newly painted with her black hull, the Gwalia *lies at the Landing Stage, Newport, on a wet day in 1906.
Visible on the waterline at her stem is the 'smudge' of mud picked up while swinging on the flood tide; a
manoeuvre whereby the vessel's bow was run into the mud of the east bank of the river. With her bow held fast,
the flow of the tide has swung her stern around. She has then backed off and drifted upstream until adjacent to
the landing stage, where, with careful use of the engines, she has been brought alongside.*

The syndicate members then published a handbill stating that they were the
owners of the *Gwalia*, *Devonia* and *Westonia*. This drew a long letter to the Bristol
Channel newspapers from Mr Bliss, Campbells' solicitor, setting out the reasons for
the interim injunction and reiterating Campbells' claim that the 'Barry & Bristol
Channel Steamship Co.' and the 'Red Funnel Line' were merely aliases for the Barry
Railway.

Although Easter Monday fell late in 1906 – on 16 April – both the White and Red
funnel companies started their Cardiff to Weston services as early as 2 April.

That season the hull colours of the Red Funnel Line were changed from light
grey to black. The reason is unknown but possibly, as in the case of the *Heather Bell*
in 1902, the Bristol pilots may have objected owing to the difficulty in seeing the
light grey hulls in poor visibility, although, like the *Heather Bell*, their funnels were
'unmissable'.

The *Westonia* had also undergone a number of alterations during the winter, the
principal of which was the removal of her raised forecastle. She ran a trial trip on 5
April 1906 and was stated to have been 'eminently satisfactory'.

It may be remembered from the previous volume that the *Cambria* had been
found a faster ship when trimmed by the head, (i.e. when her draught at the bow
was slightly greater than that at the stern). During the winter of 1905/1906 her after
lifeboat and davits were removed to enable that trim to be maintained – a course of
action which would most certainly not be allowed today!

A magnificent view of the Gwalia *at speed, passing Battery Point, Portishead, in 1906.*

Devonia *at the Porthcawl breakwater in 1906.*

Above: Gwalia *in the river Avon in 1906.*

Left: Westonia *arriving at Penarth in 1906.*

Opposite above: Cambria, *(minus her stern lifeboat), heading into the Bristol Channel from the river Avon, 1906/1908.*

Opposite below: Westward Ho *passing* Hotwells Landing Stage *to swing at* Tongue Head, *in the 1900s.*

The White Funnel steamers began their down-channel Easter sailings on Wednesday 11 April 1906 when the *Cambria*, helped by a big spring tide in both directions, made remarkable runs. Leaving Cardiff at 09.45 and calling at Penarth she reached Ilfracombe in two hours and two minutes! She sailed from Ilfracombe at 16.00, arrived at Penarth at 17.50 and was alongside the pontoon at Cardiff at 18.00, exactly two hours from Ilfracombe; a distance of forty-two nautical miles. The Red Funnel Line's first trip to Ilfracombe took place on the following day.

A major event in Bristol Channel history took place when, at just after 02.00 on Wednesday 30 May 1906, the 14,000 ton battleship, HMS *Montagu* ran ashore in dense fog close to Shutter Rock on the south-westerly corner of Lundy Island. No reports appeared in the newspapers until the following day, Thursday 31 May, and to say that the incident caused a sensation would be a gross understatement.

P&A Campbell Ltd advertised that morning in the Bristol and Cardiff newspapers that a special trip would be run that day by the *Westward Ho* to Ilfracombe and to off Lundy to view the wreck. The Red Funnel Line ran a similar trip on 1 June and on Saturday 2 June the *Devonia* left Barry at 10.10, with a connecting train from Cardiff, followed by the *Gwalia* from Cardiff Pier Head at 14.30, both bound for Ilfracombe and a cruise to see the *Montagu*. Similar afternoon trips were run on the same day by the *Britannia* and *Westward Ho,* during the course of which a westerly gale blew up. Nevertheless, all the steamers ran their advertised trips and those of their passengers not afflicted with 'mal-de-mer' were rewarded by the sight of heavy seas overwhelming the stricken battleship.

Throughout June 1906 P&A Campbell Ltd ran cruises from Bristol, Clevedon, Newport, Cardiff and Penarth, while the Red Funnel Line ran from Cardiff, Penarth and Barry to see the wreck of the *Montagu,* and then, most surprisingly, the Red Funnel Line advertised trips to Lundy 'To Land'. How this was contrived is not known for the Revd Hudson Grossett Heaven, up to that time, had permitted only the *Brighton* to land passengers, and that, at most, not more than twice a week. The Revd Heaven was now aged eighty, his health was beginning to fail and he had spent the winter of 1905/1906 on the mainland; he had also put Lundy up for sale but there had been no offers. Possibly a generous payment by the Barry Railway tempted him to grant permission for their steamers to land; this, however, is just surmise. After the landings by the Red Funnel steamers the *Brighton*'s advertisements ceased to state, 'The Only Vessel in the Bristol Channel Permitted to land Passengers at Lundy Island'.

The first Red Funnel trip to land at Lundy took place on Friday 29 June 1906 and by mid-July they were being run every other day, except Sundays, and in August every day, again except Sundays.

During June, July and August 1906 P&A Campbell Ltd made almost seventy cruises to off Lundy to view the *Montagu*. When the tide did not serve at Bristol the steamers sailed from Avonmouth, with connecting trains from Temple Meads. At Cardiff, if there was insufficient water in the mornings, the cruises started in the afternoons with consequent late returns but this did not deter passengers eager to see the wreck. Direct runs were also made from Newport, tide permitting, and the *Ilfracombe Chronicle* reported that people were flocking into Ilfracombe by rail hoping to obtain a trip by steamer out to the *Montagu*.

While the salvage operations were proceeding, Peter was presented with a small piece of brass from the wreck which he had made into a handle for the *Britannia*'s steering wheel so that it could be spun around quickly in an emergency.

The battleship, HMS Montagu, *ashore at Lundy on Thursday 31 May 1906. The White Funnel steamer passing, in the background, appears to be the* Cambria.

HMS Montagu *ashore at Lundy, with the pyramid shaped Shutter Rock behind, June 1906.*

Mumbles in 1906 with the Devonia *at the pier and the Mumbles Railway in the foreground.*

Gwalia *at anchor off Lundy in 1906.*

In the upper reaches of the channel the *Ravenswood* and *Waverley* maintained the Cardiff to Weston ferry in competition with the *Westonia*. The latter was bound for Weston on 12 July closely followed by the *Ravenswood*, which overhauled the *Westonia* a few miles from Birnbeck Pier. The piermaster hoisted the *Westonia's* flag regardless of the fact that she had now been overtaken. The *Ravenswood,* however, took the pier first and a heated argument ensued between the pier master and Capt. Chidgey; the pier master threatening to cut the *Ravenswood's* ropes. Nothing further happened on that day but eventually, through the machinations of Mr J.H. Westyr-Evans, a solicitor who had wired the Board of Trade making allegations against the

Seen from the Westward Ho *as she approaches the Pier Head, Cardiff, the* Ravenswood *departs for Weston.*

Ravenswood, the case went to court. The Stipendiary Magistrate in Cardiff favoured the *Westonia's* side of the story and fined Capt. Chidgey the maximum penalty of £100, which P&A Campbell paid. Remarks were passed during the hearing concerning 'The high feeling existing between the two companies'.

This high feeling had spilled over into another quarter when, at the end of June 1906, the *Western Mail* reported:

> White Funnel v Red Funnel Employees Squabble at Cardiff
> The rivalry between the respective owners of the White and Red Funnel lines of the Bristol Channel passenger steamers appears to have extended itself to the employees of the two companies. Before the Cardiff Stipendiary, a baggage porter employed by P&A Campbell Ltd. summoned a pontoon man of the Red Funnel Line for assault. The defendant called a fellow employee who stated that the baggage porter had started the bother by saying 'Damn fine boats you got – always breaking down'.

In contrast to the provocative nature of events in the Bristol Channel, Campbells' South Coast services with the *Brighton Queen* and *Glen Rosa* had progressed smoothly and profitably during the past few seasons; so much so that the company decided that business warranted an additional steamer, to be based at Hastings, during the height of the season. The steamer chosen was the *Bonnie Doon*, which left Bristol on 30 July 1906 bound for Southampton and Newhaven. She commenced running from Hastings on 1 August mainly to Eastbourne and Brighton besides running short cruises in the channel 'To view shipping' or around the Royal Sovereign lightvessel.

Waverley *leaving Cardiff in 1907.*

Britannia *outward bound in the river Avon in the 1900s.*

Brighton Queen *at Boulogne in the 1900s.*

Brighton Queen *leaving Boulogne in the 1900s.*

Glen Rosa *off Brighton in the 1900s.*

To return to the Bristol Channel. Both the *Gwalia* and *Cambria* were scheduled to make trips from Cardiff to Newquay on 15 August 1906. The former left Barry Pier at 07.10 direct for Ilfracombe while the latter left Cardiff at 06.00, calling at Penarth, Weston, Minehead and off Lynmouth. The *Gwalia* arrived at Ilfracombe first and was first away for Newquay. The weather on the previous day and night had been unsettled and a big swell running in the channel was added to by a strong south-westerly wind. Passengers at Ilfracombe did not seem to be deterred and about 350 joined the *Cambria*. When in sight of Hartland Point many of them were surprised to see the *Gwalia* put about and return across Bideford Bay. There had been some 'faint hearts' aboard her who had requested Capt. James to put back; he called for a show of hands and as there appeared to be a majority, he did as they asked. The *Gwalia* arrived at Ilfracombe at about 14.00 and lay at the inner berth, ahead of the Stone Bench, until her sailing time of 20.30. Despite the very heavy seas encountered by the *Cambria* neither Capt. Livingstone nor his passengers thought of turning back. Throughout the day news that the *Cambria* had gone on to Newquay spread through Ilfracombe and that night a large crowd assembled on Capstone Parade and on the pier to watch her return and cheer her on her way back to Cardiff.

Some idea of the sea conditions on that day can be gauged from the fact that the *Normandy* left Mumbles at 09.00 for Tenby and Ilfracombe, passing to the west of Lundy in order to see the wreck of the *Montagu*. The *Normandy* experienced a very bad passage and did not reach Ilfracombe until 17.00 – her scheduled time of departure. She discharged only her single journey passengers and returned immediately to Tenby where her arrival, at 21.30, was anxiously awaited by a large number of worried relatives and friends.

The *Gwalia* was chartered for the Ilfracombe Tradesmen's annual outing, to Barry, Cardiff and Bristol, on 27 September. Three hundred and twenty boarded her at Ilfracombe and she then, most unusually, stopped off Combe Martin to pick up a further forty who came out to her in boats. Both the *Gwalia* and *Cambria* made their final trips to Ilfracombe as late as 3 October 1906.

The Barry Railway was still considering new tonnage and on 10 December 1906 John Brown & Co. Ltd sent a tender to Robert Forrest, significantly, for the Barry Railway, for a duplicate of the *Gwalia* for which they quoted £31,600. A week later another tender was sent to Robert Forrest, again to the Barry Railway, this time for a duplicate of the Bangor & County Down Railway's *Slieve Bearnagh*, at £24,200. This tender was accepted and the page in Brown's tender book has written across it 'No.379 – Delivery – Midsummer 1907'.

1907

The new steamer ordered by the Barry Railway was intended to operate a summer and winter service between Barry and Burnham-on-Sea to connect with the railway network of the Somerset & Dorset Joint Railway. A Bill was to go before Parliament in 1907 and the Barry company was to provide fresh capital for the building of a pier at Burnham, the site being considered to be more sheltered in the winter than Weston. The running of this service would be quite within the limits laid down by the 1904 Act. The Barry minute books contain a paragraph which stated:

> It would not be worth the consideration of the Barry directors unless they were sure beforehand that the Somerset & Dorset Joint Railway had approved of the scheme and would endeavour to make it a success.

Although the contract for the new steamer had not yet been signed John Brown's records state, '16 January 1907. No.379. Keel blocks laid; material being ordered; preparing to commence frames'. The specifications had also been accepted and it is of interest to note that the mean draught in salt water when the vessel was ready for service, with 25 tons of deadweight – coal, water, stores and passengers – was not to exceed a shallow 5ft 9in, and that the gangways were to be 8ft 6in wide to allow cars to be shipped.

Meanwhile, litigation continued. In the Chancery Division of the High Court, on 22 January 1907, two adjourned summonses came for hearing before Mr Justice Swinfen-Eady. The action itself had not been set down for trial, the present application was on behalf of P&A Campbell Ltd for a full affidavit of documents and the power to administer interrogatories to the syndicate and to the Barry Railway Co.

Mr Micklin K.C., for P&A Campbell Ltd, stated that at the first order for discovery in February 1906, certain documents were not disclosed. It was alleged that in April 1905 the defendants, (the syndicate), in the name of the Barry & Bristol Channel Steamship Co., advertised and continued to advertise their vessels as plying inside the limits allowed by the Barry Acts. It was claimed that the Acts complained of were devised and procured by T.R. Thompson, managing director of the Barry Railway Co. Counsel submitted that to ascertain this the plaintiffs, (P&A Campbell Ltd), were entitled to see the form in which the accounts were kept but that the defendants had not disclosed the most important documents. The judge ordered a further affidavit of documents in general terms, and that the interrogatories must be answered.

On 11 February 1907 the Red Funnel Line was registered as a limited company; this was another subterfuge. The shareholders were the syndicate plus James Herbert Cory and Albert Foa, both shareholders in the Barry Railway Co. The capital of the Red Funnel Line Ltd was £30,000 in £1 shares. The members of the syndicate held 5,000 shares each but the total amount of cash received by the company in respect of the shares issued wholly for cash was nil; the shares issued partly for cash was also nil; in other words, no actual shares were ever issued.

The Easter weekend of 1907 saw a number of untoward incidents. On Easter Saturday 30 March the *Gwalia* left Cardiff at 17.40 with 400 passengers for Clevedon and Bristol. While rounding the Horseshoe Bend in the river Avon, the strong flood tide forced her on to the mud of the Gloucestershire bank, considerably damaging her port paddle wheel. Fortunately a tug was in the river which towed her into the Cumberland Basin. Two Barry tugs later towed her to Barry for repairs but the Red Funnel sailings from Bristol on Easter Monday and Tuesday were cancelled.

On the morning of Easter Monday the *Albion* left Newport for Bristol at the early hour of 06.45 in very dense fog. She touched a mud bank in the river Usk on her way down to the sea and then crept across the channel at very slow speed. Her master, Capt. James Nurcombe Webber, kept the lead swinging all the way across to check the depth of water beneath her but suddenly the ship took to the ground. The strong ebb tide had set her further east than Capt. Webber anticipated but with remarkable luck the *Albion* had run aground on a clear shingle patch between two outcrops of rock. The fog lifted shortly afterwards when she was seen to be about 30 yards south of the Blacknore Lighthouse. As soon as the tide had left her, a gangway was put down from the foredeck to the beach and her passengers were able to walk ashore. Those who could afford to took cabs to Portishead station, those who could not had to walk, but all were returned to Newport by train at the company's expense. When the tide served that evening the *Albion* came off the beach with the assistance of seven tugs as the clock on the nearby Portishead Nautical School struck nine. She was towed to Bristol and entered Stothert's Dry Dock for survey where the damage was found to be only superficial.

The *Albion's* passengers were not the only ones to be disappointed; there were a further 800 waiting at Newport for the *Ravenswood* to take them to Weston and Ilfracombe. She had come up from Cardiff on the previous evening and anchored for the night just below the mouth of the Usk. In the morning Capt. Chidgey considered it too dangerous to journey up river and stayed where he was. The trip was cancelled and the *Ravenswood* returned to Cardiff later in the day.

Above and below:
Albion *ashore near
Blacknore Point,
Portishead, on Easter
Monday 1 April 1907.*

Devonia in the river Avon in 1907.

The new landing stage at the Grand Pier, Weston-super-Mare, was opened for steamer traffic on the evening of 16 May 1907; the *Ravenswood,* dressed overall, doing the honours. As the steamer came alongside, Mrs J.H. Stevenson, wife of the pier manager, cut a ribbon releasing a bottle of champagne which neatly smashed itself against the pier piles.

The building of the Grand Pier had commenced in 1903 and the first section, containing the pavilion, was opened during the following year. The pier was extended during 1904/1907 and was then almost three quarters of a mile long, but still not far enough out to sea to enable the steamers to use it at all states of the tide. A further extension of another quarter of a mile was to be added but this never materialised. The White Funnel steamers called at the Grand Pier on four occasions during 1907, the Red Funnel steamers seven. All of the calls were made on spring tides and usually in the evenings.

The new pier at Chepstow was opened on the arrival of the *Cambria* on Thursday 23 May 1907. Although a very modest little pier it was a great improvement on the previous facilities – a somewhat decrepit barge which rose and fell with the tide and which was joined to the river bank by a crude gangway. P&A Campbell Ltd took the opportunity of reviving trips from Chepstow to Weston and Ilfracombe in connection with GWR trains from Gloucester via all the Forest of Dean stations, as they had done in the 1890s.

Three steamers were again to be based on the South Coast for the season, as in 1906 – the *Brighton Queen, Glen Rosa* and *Bonnie Doon.* The latter had undergone a number of alterations during the winter. A shorter, larger diameter funnel replaced the tall thin one, and she was plated in forward of the funnel with a door each side leading out on to the foredeck.

Cambria *at the opening of the new pier at Chepstow on Thursday 23 May 1907.*

The subject of this photograph, taken in Bristol during the winter of 1906/1907, was the tug, and her crew, but an enlargement of the background shows the Ravenswood, *(left), and* Bonnie Doon *in the Merchant's Dock. The* Bonnie Doon *has just been fitted with her new, larger diameter funnel.*

Bonnie Doon *at Newhaven, 1907/1910.*

Aboard Bonnie Doon *on the South Coast, 1907/1910.*

Capt. John West on the bridge of the Brighton Queen.

Bonnie Doon *leaving Brighton,* 1907/1910.

Contrasting vessels at John Brown's yard, Clydebank, in April 1907. To the left – the Cunard liner Lusitania *fitting out, and centre – No.379 under construction.*

The launch of the Barry, *4 May 1907.*

The Barry Railway's new steamer – No.379 – was launched at John Brown's yard, Clydebank on 4 May 1907 by Robert Forrest's daughter, Nesta, who christened the vessel *Barry*. The *Western Mail* made an unfortunate faux pas by printing in its report of the launch that the *Barry* belonged to the Red Funnel Line when, in fact, she legitimately belonged to the Barry Railway. A hasty apology and correction appeared in the following issue.

Above: *The* Barry *on trials in the Firth of Clyde on 31 May 1907. The white band on the funnel, the white line above the red boot topping and the Barry Railway Co.'s house flag were intended to emphasise the fact that she was owned by the Barry Railway and not the syndicate.*

Right: *The* Barry *fitting out at John Brown's yard in May 1907.*

The Barry *leaving Barry in 1907.*

The *Barry* ran her preliminary trials on 24 May and her official trials, at Skelmorlie, on 31 May, her best speed being 17.5 knots and her mean speed 17.31 knots. Her hull form, as far as the underbody was concerned, was a duplicate of the *Slieve Bearnagh,* like hers, very fine lined, the *Barry,* however, had much greater sheer and her bows had considerably more flare. The hull too, was strengthened for the proposed winter service.

The after deckhouse had wings extending to the inboard faces of the paddle boxes and the engine room skylight was positioned up on the forward end of the deckhouse. A circular skylight on the after end of the promenade deck gave light to the main saloon.

The boiler, as in the *Slieve Bearnagh,* was double ended with the uptakes leading into one funnel, but the *Barry's* boiler was 3in longer and 9in greater in diameter; the working pressure being the same in both vessels at 150 per square inch. Their engines were identical in size and stroke.

The *Slieve Bearnagh* had seven float paddle wheels with wooden floats whereas the *Barry,* unusually for a Clydebank paddler, had eight float wheels with steel floats. The devices on her paddle boxes were the arms of the Barry Railway.

The *Barry* wore a white band on her funnel between the red and black to denote the supposedly different ownership from the Red Funnel Line. She also had a white ribbon above the red boot topping, a feature which was incorporated into the *Gwalia, Devonia* and *Westonia* from the 1907 season.

The woodwork in the *Barry,* particularly in the main saloon, was of the very finest walnut and mahogany. This was fitted following a miscalculation by her builders.

While the *Barry* was under construction the Cunard liner, *Lusitania*, was being built in the next yard. John Brown's over estimated the quantities of wood required for the Cunarder and that which was spare was worked into the *Barry*.

The ship presented a very handsome appearance, so much so that Capt. Peter, on seeing her coming up river to Bristol, made the prophetic remark, 'That is the prettiest paddler I have ever seen. I would like to own her myself'.

The *Barry* left Clydebank on 4 June 1907 under the command of Capt. George Ayland, an old Bristol Channel hand, and arrived in Barry Dock on the following day. Her first trip took place on Saturday 15 June from Barry to Minehead, Weston and return. Her sailings were advertised separately from the Red Funnel Line and were headed:

BARRY RAILWAY COMPANY
Regular Service to Minehead, Weston and Clevedon; Watchet and Minehead.
Via Cardiff Riverside Station and Barry Pier.

The Red Funnel Line had not ventured further than Newquay for their long distance excursions but on Friday 21 June 1907 they began a weekend trip to Penzance and the Isles of Scilly by the *Gwalia*. The *Normandy* ran a special trip from Swansea to connect with her at Ilfracombe, about forty passengers booking through from Swansea at 24*s* return.

Dining saloon of the Gwalia.

The Barry *embarking passengers at Lynmouth in 1907.*

Right to left: Barry, Devonia *and* Westonia *at Barry in 1907. Before the beginning of that season the*
Gwalia, Devonia *and* Westonia *were painted with a white line above the boot topping. A close look at the*
photograph reveals that the white band around the Barry's *funnel is being repainted, as if the Barry Railway*
were ensuring that the difference in ownership would not pass un-noticed.

The Barry *at the Stone Bench, Ilfracombe, on a windy day in 1907.*

The Barry *leaving Minehead pier in 1907.*

Behind the scenes litigation continued. On 21 June Mr Eve KC, on behalf of the Barry Railway, made an application in the Court of Chancery for a claim of inspection of documents held by P&A Campbell Ltd. This was granted and the trial of the action was set down for 9 July 1907.

When the trial opened the Barry Railway, P&A Campbell Ltd, and T.R. Thompson and the syndicate were each represented by three KC's. The Action was – The Attorney General at the relation of P&A Campbell Ltd v the Barry Railway and others.

In opening his case Mr Micklen KC said that the Barry Railway obtained Parliamentary powers under which they purchased the *Gwalia* and *Devonia*. Then an arrangement was alleged by the plaintiffs, P&A Campbell Ltd, to have been made between the Barry Railway and the syndicate. The defendants, the Barry Railway, had made a statement that the ships had been bought by the syndicate and a cheque was produced, but later it appeared that the real arrangement was one under which the syndicate was entirely in the hands of the Barry Railway and that the ships, instead of having been purchased, had not had a farthing paid for them, and remained the property of the railway company.

What the plaintiffs asked for was:

A declaration that the registration of the ships in question in the names of the first four defendants, Symonds, North Lewis, Rees Jones and Radford, was a colourable and fraudulent device on the part of the defendants.

A declaration that the defendant company had acted *ultra vires* in ordering and contracting to purchase the ships named and also in promoting a syndicate to run them.

A declaration that the transfer of the *Gwalia* and *Devonia* into the names of Symonds, North Lewis, Rees Jones and Radford, and the registration of the *Westonia* in the same names enabled the defendants company to exceed their powers.

An injunction restraining all the defendants, their servants or agents from running the steamers except within the limits laid down by Clause 4 of the 1904 Act, and an injunction against the Barry Railway restraining them from directly or indirectly applying monies or embarking credit of that company for the purpose of providing steamers not intended to be used by the Barry company bona fide, and within the limits of the 1904 Act.

Capt. Alec, giving evidence at the commencement of the Action, said that it was common knowledge in Cardiff by whom the ships were run and owned. Asked what was the difference between the Red Funnel Line's opposition and any other competition, Alec replied, 'When you see men running expensive boats at fares that it is impossible to make pay, you cannot call it legitimate competition'.

At the second day's hearing Mr George Coates, an accountant, said that he had visited Cardiff to inspect the defendants' books but that when he requested a cash book, and the books from which the balance sheets had been drawn up, they were refused. The 1905 and 1906 agreements provided that the syndicate should receive remuneration of £10 to £15 for each trip should 25 per cent of the booking amount to that. The syndicate was to be guaranteed for all losses by the Barry Railway but the profits, after payment of an agreed remuneration to the syndicate, were to belong to the Barry Railway. Also that the latter were to have power to resume the steamers at any time they thought fit.

The judge commented that the statutory services for 1905 showed a loss of £1,233 which was borne by the Barry Co. and that it was a curious thing that the Barry Co. should pay all losses if the syndicate were carrying on business for themselves.

On the third day of the hearing Mr Micklen took the unprecedented step of placing Mr William Mein, the secretary of the Barry Railway, in the witness box as a witness for the plaintiffs. Under cross examination Mr Mein said that he could not say who made the arrangements with Mr Symonds as to the steamers. He could find nothing in the minute books with reference to those arrangements; they would have been made verbally between the directors and Mr Symonds.

A letter had been received from John Brown & Co. Ltd pressing for payment of an instalment on the *Gwalia* and *Devonia*. Mr Micklen then stated, 'And it was resolved to pay them £9,558 in April 1905, notwithstanding the fact that the steamers had supposedly been disposed of some considerable time before?' Mr Mein replied 'Yes'.

Mr Warmington KC, for the plaintiffs said that he had only just received extracts from the Barry Railway minute books, and that they merely gave him particular dates without any statements as to who was present at the meetings. The judge then stated that the lack of this information was quite unpardonable; the plaintiffs had been labouring under great disadvantages and had not had the discovery to which they were entitled. He adjourned the case until 22 July by which time the full entries in the minute books were to be produced.

Before the adjourned trial re-commenced, counsel for the defendants advised the Barry Railway and the syndicate that, following the disclosures from the minute books, their defence must collapse and strongly urged them to submit to a settlement and accept the injunction.

The injunction to which the Barry Railway submitted was expressed in more stringent terms than was even asked for in the plaintiffs' Statement of Claim, and was prefaced by an admission that the steamers were, and always had been their property, notwithstanding their previous denials.

In accordance with the injunction, the Barry Railway agreed that under the terms of the agreements of March 1905 and January 1906 as to the incorporation of the Red Funnel Line, the three steamers remained their property. They also agreed that the defendants T.R. Thompson and all others, the directors, servants and agents of the Barry Railway, either directly in the name of the company or indirectly in the

Departures from the Pier Head, Cardiff, in 1907.

Devonia leaving Cardiff prior to 31 July 1907. (The syndicate's flag is being flown below the name pendant on her foremast). She is therefore defying the restrictions of Clause 4 of the Barry Railway (Steam vessels) Act, of 1904. And so is the Gwalia which can be seen on the right, lying at the Pier Head. The White Funnel steamers just visible behind the Devonia are (left) Cambria *and (right)* Ravenswood.

Photographed a little later on the same day, the Cambria *departs with a good complement of passengers.*

Followed by the Ravenswood.

And finally the Gwalia.

names of the defendants Symonds, North Lewis, Rees Jones and Radford, should be restrained from running steamers except within the limits authorised by Clause 4 of the Barry (Steam Vessels) Act of 1904.

The Barry company agreed to pay the plaintiffs' costs which amounted to £8,000, including the costs of the three counsel. Their own costs amounted to £5,916 making a total of £13,916 – an exceedingly high sum of money in 1907!

The effects of the injunction were to completely shut out the Barry Railway steamers from Cardiff, Penarth and Newport. They could run to Clevedon and Bristol provided that they only carried passengers there and back and did not embark fresh passengers at either place. P&A Campbell Ltd agreed to withhold enforcement of the injunction until 31 July 1907 as the defendants' timetables had been made up to that date. Thereafter their sailings were to be amended accordingly.

'Red Funnel Line' sailings were advertised up to 31 July but on the following day the adverts were changed to 'Barry Railway Company' with 'Red Funnel Line' underneath in much smaller letters. The adverts also stressed 'All sailings after 31 July 1907 are from Barry Pier only, via train from Riverside Station, Cardiff.' There was no increase in fares, which now included rail tickets from Cardiff.

Another change which occurred after 31 July was that the Barry steamers wore the Barry Railway's houseflag which had previously only been seen on the *Barry*. The Barry

Red Funnel personnel photographed on the Gwalia. *Capt. James W. James is seated in the centre, with Chief Officer Hoskins on his right. On Capt. James's left is Chief Engineer Black with Second Engineer Wilson next to him.*

Gwalia *entering the river Avon, 1907/1909.*

& Bristol Channel Steamship Co. had a very large white pendant with the Prince of Wales' feathers in red upon it. The Barry Railway pendant was much smaller; the hoist half was white, with the red Barry dragon superimposed, and the fly half was red.

The half-yearly meeting of the Barry Railway shareholders was held on 2 August 1907. The newspaper headlines stated:

BARRY COMPANY MEETING.
A SHAREHOLDER AND THE CHANNEL BOATS.
CRITICAL AND INSISTENT OBSERVATIONS.

The *South Wales Daily News* gave an almost verbatim report of the meeting which, at times, reached farcical proportions owing to the 'critical and insistent observations' of Lt-Col. E.P. Clarke of Bristol.

T.R. Thompson was in the chair and said at the outset that he would simply pass one remark with regard to the steamer. Action which all present knew the company had been engaged in for some time. The court had decided that the much appreciated steamer service was not within the scope of the company's powers, and in those circumstances the boats were now running within the prescribed limits. 'Quite right', interjected Col. Clarke. Mr Thompson then stated, 'I don't know why that gentleman says "Quite right"', to which Col. Clarke replied, 'Because I don't believe in running them at all'.

Mr Thompson then stated that the Burnham Pier Bill had been passed by Parliament and it was hoped that when the pier had been constructed it would be the means of bringing passengers and other traffic over the Barry Railways.

To Mr Thompson's increasing annoyance, a continual stream of interruptions and questions came from Col. Clarke who said that he had written to the Barry company's secretary on 29 May 1905, stating that he hoped the company would not start running pleasure steamers. He had received a reply dating from the following day which stated:

> The steamers to which you refer were built to the order of this company and transferred to a separate company at the same price. The cost thereof will not appear in the Barry Company's accounts.

Col. Clarke then continued:

> I have been reading through this unfortunate trial and it seems to me that this statement was a mistake because the boats belong to the Barry Co. at the present time, so how could it be said next day to that on which I wrote that they had been transferred to a separate company? But they have come back again. Why don't they admit that they are their property?

Mr Thompson side-stepped these two questions but in reply to Col. Clarke's next question which asked whether the transfer was a bona fide transaction, Mr Thompson made the astounding statement that it was! To which Col. Clarke retorted, 'But you have got them back again. Are they the company's steamships or not?'

Mr Thompson replied, 'They are, or will be, but up to the present moment the company have not paid for them'.

This was another astonishing remark in view of the fact that at the close of the Action the Barry Railway had admitted that the steamers were, and always had been their property, notwithstanding their previous denials.

Col. Clarke continued:

> I get up here to represent my family who have a good deal of money in this concern... I look upon passenger steamers as being no part of a railway company's undertaking. First these boats were christened the Barry and Bristol Channel Steamship Co. and then they are re-christened the Red Funnel Line, and then we have an action brought against the company which will mean many hundreds. I was very sorry to see it for I was hoping they had been got rid of. I think it would be very much better if they had let the steamers alone. With regard to the £9,000 for the Burnham Pier, I hope they will think twice before they spend that money. I would far sooner give it to the hospital or to the sick fund of the men than throw it away like that because you will never see a penny piece of it. I think our report should contain something of the profit and loss of these steamers. We are all anxious to make the trade of Barry prosperous and I have no fault to find with the directors, but I think we might have a fuller report and if it had not been for Campbells' Action many of us would never have known a word about this transaction with these boats at all.

Mr Thompson replied:

I do not like to interrupt you but you really are taking up the time of the meeting – a very considerable time. Whatever has been done in respect of these steamers has been done under the very best legal advice and the directors have acted in the very best interest of the shareholders. I submit that there is absolutely nothing in that report which entitles you to get up and pass the comments you are passing.

A further altercation then followed in which Col. Clarke stated that he did not think the steamers would ever pay; he had invested money in a good, going railway concern and not in a precarious traffic, like steamers, to which Mr Thompson replied that he put no value on Col. Clarke's opinion whatever, and ended by saying. 'I do not suppose we will follow your advice. I am not enamoured with it'.

Although Col. Clarke was still not satisfied with the explanation of the handling of the steamer business, Mr Thompson's final remarks appear to have silenced him.

A notable event of the 1907 season was the opening of the Queen Alexandra Dock, Cardiff, on 13 July, by King Edward VII and Queen Alexandra. The Royal Yacht, *Victoria and Albert,* and a naval escort arrived in the channel on the previous evening and were escorted from Breaksea Point by the *Cambria, Gwalia* and *Barry.* The newspapers reported that Queen Alexandra could be clearly seen on deck, taking photographs. The opening ceremony was described as:

> …a colourful and exciting affair with crowds of people, 6,000 invited guests, long lines of bunting and bands playing. The pleasure steamers were in attendance in Cardiff Roads and even the tugs and dredgers were dressed overall.

The Royal Yacht, Victoria and Albert, *at the entrance to Cardiff Docks on the evening of 12 July 1907.*

Gwalia *arriving at Ilfracombe. 1907/1909.*

An innovation of the 1907 season was that of day trips to St Ives. The *Gwalia* was the first to visit the Cornish resort on Friday 19 July, leaving Barry at 06.30 and returning at 16.30, having afforded her passengers two and a half hours ashore.

Campbells followed suit on Monday 19 August, leaving Cardiff at the early hour of 03.30 via Weston, Lynmouth and Ilfracombe. On the forward journey the passengers had to wait for two hours at Ilfracombe to change into the *Britannia*, which came down from Bristol and Clevedon. On the return journey the Clevedon and Bristol passengers had to change into the *Westward Ho* at Ilfracombe. She was alongside Clevedon Pier at midnight when a most unfortunate accident happened. The passengers had been landed, the gangways hauled in and the ropes about to be cast off when the main steam pipe from the boiler to the engines split in the stokehold, filling the main saloon and the after part of the ship with steam. Panic was averted by Capt. Dan Taylor and the mate, Geordie Campbell, (no relation to Peter and Alec).

Two firemen were badly scalded and were taken to the Clevedon Cottage Hospital but there were no other casualties. Meanwhile, a telephone message from the office on Clevedon Pier summoned the *Ravenswood* from Cardiff. Fortunately she still had steam up and arrived alongside the *Westward Ho* at Clevedon at 02.00 on Tuesday 20 August and took the remaining passengers on to Bristol. The *Westward Ho* was towed to Bristol later that morning and ended her season.

The *Devonia* also ran into difficulties on her return from Ilfracombe on 2 October 1907 when she smashed one of her paddle floats on partly submerged wreckage while passing the Foreland at about 19.30. She drifted up channel with the tide to off Minehead and then across to the vicinity of the Breaksea Lightvessel. In response to her distress rockets the tugs *Windsor* and *Clive* put out from Barry and towed her in, arriving at 00.50 on the following morning.

Waverley *at the Landing Stage, Newport, in the 1900s.*

Cambria *arriving at Ilfracombe, 1906/1908. It appears that she has experienced a rough trip down channel judging by the surf breaking on the rocks below Hillsborough and, more significantly, the fact that wooden weatherboards have been shipped on the six forward windows of the* Cambria's *forward saloon. This is the only known photograph of a White Funnel steamer so fitted.*

With the island of Samson in the background, the Britannia *leaves Hughtown, St Mary's, Isles of Scilly, in 1907.*

Westward Ho *passing Battery Point, Portishead, in the 1900s.*

Capt. Dan Taylor and Chief Officer James Bilson, (at the wheel), aboard Britannia, *at Ilfracombe in the 1900s.*

The deck crew and a fireman (right) of the Britannia *at Ilfracombe .*

Left to right: Brighton, Normandy *and* Gwalia *at Ilfracombe in 1907.*

P&A Campbell ran their last trip of the season to Ilfracombe on 4 October but the Barry steamers continued until 7 October. Campbells' last trips from Cardiff to Weston were on 12 October but the last trips from Barry to Weston had taken place on 7 October 1907.

Capt. Allan Livingstone of the *Cambria* appeared before a special sitting of Bristol magistrates on 25 November 1907. It was alleged that he was guilty of an infringement of the Regulations Preventing Collision at Sea by not keeping the *Cambria* clear of the *Devonia* on 30 August 1907 while both vessels were following a race of pilot cutters off Barry.

Counsel for Capt. Livingstone expressed regret that the charge had been made the subject of criminal proceedings. He thought a better plan would have been to have held a court of inquiry before the local Marine Board, when both parties would have been in the same position. Instead of that the charge was made a criminal one and colouring was given by the owners of the Red Funnel Line. They had been in competition with P&A Campbell Ltd and sought reprisal against them. He failed to see why the Barry Railway should be brought into the matter at all and alleged that they were not content to leave it to the Board of Trade.

After a three-day hearing the magistrates dismissed the three charges and awarded Capt. Livingstone £20 costs on each of the first two.

Bad news was imparted to the Barry Railway company's directors on 6 December 1907, when the general manager informed them that the Bridgewater Port & Navigation Authority were applying for a Provisional Order under which they would be able to charge increased dues on a vessel and for mooring vessels within the area of their authority. This would enable them to make increased charges for the traffic at Burnham Pier. They were also seeking powers to use an 'Eroder' which might have the effect of causing a deposit of silt at or about Burnham. Both propositions would have adverse effects on the proposed Barry to Burnham service.

DARING AND DEFEAT

1908

As there was no need for further evasion or camouflage, the *Gwalia*, *Devonia* and *Westonia* were re-registered in the ownership of the Barry Railway on 22 January 1908, and during the winter the *Barry* had the white band on her funnel painted out.

The *Westonia* underwent considerable alterations. Several feet were cut off her funnels, her saloons were extended to the full width of the ship and refurbished, while the companionways on the after sponsons were decked over.

There had been considerable criticism in the Cardiff newspapers of the Barry Railway's handling of their steamer problem. Mr T.R. Thompson made a lengthy speech at the half-yearly meeting of shareholders on 7 February 1908, in reply to what he termed:

> The recent attack and virulent opposition and criticism in the press on the policy of the directors... I wish to deal with the attempts that have been made, and which are being continued, to impede the Barry Co's. progress by people who hope to secure for themselves the practical monopoly of the steamship service in the Bristol Channel.

He then made a bitter attack on P&A Campbell Ltd, distorting their request in 1900 for the receipts to be made up to £6,500 per season, as 'an exorbitant demand'. He complained that Campbells 'greatly prejudiced the success of the service by filling the steamers with passengers before calling at Barry in 1901 and 1902'. Nothing was said about the heavy losses sustained by Campbells in running out of Barry, nor of the tremendous drop in passengers out of Barry during those years.

Mr J.B Ferrier referred to 'the mistake of the directors in taking up the steamship service', and urged them 'to wipe out their £100,000 mistake'. He continued:

> If it is for the purpose of continuing the use of the pontoons that the boats are to be worked I would prefer that the boats should be sent out into the channel and blown to pieces!

The four Red Funnel steamers in their winter quarters – the Barry Dock basin – at the end of the 1907 season.

The Barry Dock basin in the spring of 1908. The Westonia, *just visible in the middle distance, minus her funnels, is undergoing extensive alterations.*

Devonia arriving at Ilfracombe in 1908.

The chairman, the Earl of Plymouth, (formerly Lord Windsor), pointed out that the questions involved in the retention of the steamboat service was that of the passenger traffic of the company, and he confidently believed that the directors could make their steamboat service pay and be a valuable addition to their receipts.

An extraordinary meeting of shareholders then followed to consider and approve a Bill which the company then had going through Parliament. The major part of this Bill was concerned with railway business and the company's attempts to gain running powers over even more of the South Wales railway network, but a part of it was concerned with the notion of the company subscribing to the Weston, Minehead and Ilfracombe piers. This was a blatant attempt to secure majority holdings in those piers so that the pier dues payable by P&A Campbell Ltd would be so greatly increased as to render the White Funnel steamers' calling at them unprofitable. The Ilfracombe Council, who had acquired the pier in 1907, were so concerned that they appointed legal representatives in London to monitor the progress of the Bill through Parliament.

The 1908 season began with Campbells' Cardiff to Weston service on Saturday 11 April and the Barry steamers' Barry to Weston service on Monday 13 April.

During the Easter period a dredger was at work around the landing stage and approaches of the Grand Pier, Weston, in the hope of increasing the depth of water available for the steamers. It was, however, a futile operation, the mud being washed back by the tide almost as soon as it had been removed.

The Barry steamers made seven calls at the Grand Pier during 1908. It should have been eight but the visit scheduled for 17 August had to be cancelled when the *Gwalia* broke down on the way from Barry. Her passengers were transferred to the *Devonia* in mid-channel and were landed at Birnbeck Pier instead.

Above and left: *Alongside the* Devonia *at Ilfracombe Pier in 1908. The photographs were taken from the* Brighton Queen, *while making a brief call on her way from Bristol to Brighton.*

Westward Ho *being manoeuvred from the Stone Bench to the face of lfracombe pier on an ebb tide, in the* 1900s.

Capt. Joe Ashford on the bridge of the Westward Ho *in the 1900s.*

P&A Campbell Ltd made only one trip to the Grand Pier during the season, on 17 July, after which Alec refused to allow his steamers to call unless the pier was extended beyond low water.

Following the bursting of the *Westward Ho*'s main steam pipe on 19 August 1907, a subsequent inspection by the insurance company found that she was in need of a new boiler. The replacement, paid for by the underwriters, had been ordered from Hutson's and was ready for installation in the spring of 1908. She was towed from Bristol by Guy's tug *White Rose* on 8 May and arrived in Glasgow just over fifty-six hours later. The work having been completed, she ran trials on 26 May easily maintaining her original trial speed and sailed from Glasgow on the following day, arriving in Bristol on 28 May.

After a taste of being excluded from Cardiff in August and September 1907 the Barry Railway found themselves in something of a quandary in 1908. As Cardiff was closed to them efforts were made to find passengers from other sources. In June one of their steamers, usually the *Barry*, was stationed at Ilfracombe, lying up there overnight and running early trips to Clovelly, Tenby, Lynmouth and Minehead. By so doing she was able to skim off the bulk of the Ilfracombe passengers before the arrival of the Cardiff and Bristol steamers. Coaling was done at the Stone Bench, wagons bringing the coal from the cove on the opposite side of the harbour.

Britannia *off Lynmouth in the 1900s.*

The *Gwalia*, incidentally, made an unusual visit from Barry Pier on Friday 10 July when her Ilfracombe trip was extended to Appledore, the fishing and shipbuilding village at the mouth of the river Torridge. Passengers had about two hours ashore and were landed and embarked in small boats.

July 6 1908 saw the commencement of a series of trips by the Barry steamers from Mumbles Pier to Tenby. Advertisements appeared in the Swansea newspapers:

BARRY RAILWAY (RED FUNNEL STEAMERS).
SAILINGS FROM SWANSEA (WEST PIER) AND MUMBLES PIER BY THE
MAGNIFICENT SALOON STEAMERS GWALIA, DEVONIA AND BARRY.
The Fastest and Finest Steamers plying in the Bristol Channel.
Speed 21 knots.

The West Pier berth referred to in the advertisements was a set of wooden steps on the West Pier formerly used by the *Normandy*. That vessel was laid up in the South Dock at the end of the 1907 season and her owner, the Swansea solicitor J.R. Richards, was being sought by the police following the exposure of a series of malpractices which caused him to abscond to Portugal.

During the first week of July 1908 the Ilfracombe Council was surprised to receive a letter from the Barry Railway which stated:

We have been approached to run passenger steamers from Barry Pier on Sundays during the present season. Will you be kind enough to let me know that if the company decides to comply with this suggestion whether your pier will be available on Sundays...

This, to put it mildly, caused uproar in the council! The clerk pointed out that they had no powers to stop the steamers running on Sundays but the council most strongly objected. Protest meetings were held in Ilfracombe to support the council's action in objecting to the proposal; the Ilfracombe Advertising Association sent a strongly worded letter of objection to the Barry secretary, and Archbishop Seymour described the running of steamers on Sundays as 'A calamity!' Needless to say, in the face of such strong opposition the Barry company dropped its proposal.

The *Devonia* ran a day trip from Swansea and Mumbles to Ilfracombe from the West Pier steps on 14 July. She had come down light from Barry that morning and returned light the same evening so a good deal of fuel was expended for no financial gain. The *Barry* was next to run from Swansea, on 18 July, for a day trip to Weston. She too sailed light between Barry and Swansea morning and evening.

As they had done in 1905, the Swansea Harbour Trust, always very distrustful of the Barry company's intentions, charged £5 each time a Barry steamer made fast. This effectively stopped the Barry steamers from using Swansea and the remainder of the trips for that season were from Mumbles Pier only. None were to Ilfracombe but Tenby was visited every two or three days.

Above and below: *Aboard the* Barry *on a rough day, 1908/1910.*

The *Barry* had made a return trip from Avonmouth to Ilfracombe on 9 July 1908. This was the last straw for P&A Campbell Ltd who immediately went to court asking for a Writ of Sequestration, claiming that the Barry company were defying the Injunction of 1907.

The Motion came up in the Court of Chancery on 29 July 1908, before Mr Justice Swinfen-Eady. A great deal of complex legal wrangling took place at the hearing during which many of the arguments already related in this narrative were, once again, brought before the court. His Lordship, however, refused the Motion.

A sensation was caused at the Cardiff Stock Exchange on 1 August by the announcement that the dividend of the Barry Railway for the past year would be at the rate of 6.5 per cent on the Ordinary Stock. This was equivalent to only 2.5 per cent on the Deferred Ordinary Stock and was the lowest dividend since 1901. It was strongly felt that the company's steamer services had again been an important factor in reducing the dividend. Severe criticism by the shareholders was expressed at the half-yearly meeting on 7 August 1908, during which several people exhorted the directors to abandon the services altogether. The chairman stated that the boats were being run for experience and it was from this point of view that the directors hoped to benefit. At the close of the season they would be able to judge what changes, if any, should be made to the steamer services.

It will be remembered that the Barry Railway wished the Somerset & Dorset Railway to join their Burnham Pier scheme; the former company putting in a contribution of £15,000. The Somerset & Dorset, however, refused. Furthermore, the expected silting up of the pier site had already commenced. P&A Campbell Ltd made only one trip to Burnham in 1908 and the Barry steamers only two, a morning and afternoon trip on 22 August.

The *Devonia* ran into trouble on Saturday 29 August 1908. She had left Barry for Ilfracombe at 15.00 and just after passing Watermouth, a few miles east of Ilfracombe, one of the floats in the starboard paddle wheel was damaged by floating wreckage. She crawled into Ilfracombe where her engineers tried, without success, to repair the float. The *Barry* was wired for but did not arrive until 22.45 and after embarking the *Devonia*'s passengers arrived at Barry at 02.00 on the following day.

The trials and tribulations of the Bristol Channel business contrasted drastically with the smooth running of P&A Campbell's South Coast services until, on 22 August 1908, a surprising and intriguing development was announced in the *Eastbourne Chronicle*:

> We hear that the *Cambria*, a well known steamer of the *Brighton Queen* type, will shortly arrive from Bristol and will be worked in conjunction with the three other steamers now running here. A number of special excursions are being arranged

It will be asked why the *Cambria* was being sent around to the South Coast so late in the season? The answer was that she could not be spared from her

Left to right: Barry, Devonia *and* Gwalia *at Barry, 1908/1909.*

Cambria *in the river Avon, 1908.*

Photographed from a White Funnel steamer, the Devonia *arrives off Ilfracombe, 1907/1911.*

Bristol Channel duties during the busy months of July and August. It will also be asked why she was being sent to the South Coast anyway? Much speculation has been made about this question, several sources stating that she was to replace the *Bonnie Doon* which had broken down, but the simple answer, confirmed by Mr W.A. Pelly, Campbells' Eastbourne agent from 1905 to 1939, was to 'run off' a competitor.

Richard Ragsdale Collard had bought the former Clyde paddle steamer *Lady Rowena* from her Naples owners early in 1908 and based her at Newhaven. She ran principally from Hastings and Eastbourne; the *Eastbourne Chronicle* referring to her as 'The Hastings Boat'. Hastings was the station of the *Bonnie Doon* so P&A Campbell Ltd did not welcome the intrusion, especially as the *Lady Rowena* wore a white funnel in an attempt to persuade the public that she was a Campbell steamer.

The *Lady Rowena* has been described as 'Probably superior to the *Bonnie Doon*'. Perhaps this is correct with regard to her accommodation but certainly not in the matter of speed. Although the *Bonnie Doon* was no 'flier', the *Lady Rowena* was, at that time, painfully slow. On Thursday 20 August 1908 she left Eastbourne for Folkestone an hour and a half before the *Brighton Queen,* but the latter overhauled her a mile from Folkestone and berthed first.

Much has been written about the *Cambria*'s epic trip south, part of it somewhat exaggerated. It was not 'A near disaster' – the *Cambria* appeared in Lloyds Casualties with the laconic sentence 'Some slight damage to deck fittings'. It was, however, an extremely rough trip and is worthy of detailed description.

A white funnelled steamer but not a White Funnel steamer. Aboard the Lady Rowena *on the South Coast in 1908.*

It was advertised as:

A Special Cheap Trip to Southampton and Brighton. (Down by boat, back by rail). Monday 31 August by PS *Cambria*. Leave Bristol 7.30am, Cardiff 9.25am, Penarth 9.35am. Return fare 22/6. Single 10/-.

As usual, full use was made of the *Cambria's* outward passage; a return trip was advertised at the same times to Minehead, Lynmouth, Ilfracombe and Clovelly, those passengers returning in the evening in the *Westward Ho.*

The *Cambria* arrived at Ilfracombe shortly before noon, embarked her Clovelly passengers and sailed at 12.45. About thirty passengers were left on board for Southampton when she left Clovelly at 14.15.

She rounded Hartland Point and began her journey down the coast with the wind and sea rising, and the barometer falling. Little did her personnel realise that she was steaming straight into the path of a severe storm which was rapidly sweeping westward across the Atlantic Ocean. A very heavy sea quickly arose and although slowed down, the *Cambria* was shipping green seas which washed deck seats down the foredeck and smashed them against the rails. Wooden weatherboards had been shipped on the fore saloon windows but one was washed away and the glass stove in. A terrific crash from below signalled the overturning of the large sideboard and tables in the dining saloon accompanied by the sound of smashing crockery. One of the first casualties among the passengers was a doctor who was thrown down the after companionway and sustained a broken arm. The *South Wales Daily News* later commented, under the heading 'Cambria's Buffeting – Described by a Passenger':

> ...before Lands End was reached the boat tossed and rolled in such a manner as to make the passengers very uncomfortable. With the setting in of darkness the storm further increased so that the gallant little boat was being tossed about like a cockleshell and few of even the seasoned passengers could retain their legs on deck.

Capt. Allan Livingstone, who shared with Peter, Alec and Dan Taylor the reputation of never having put back for stress of weather, decided to carry on, for Padstow, Hayle and St Ives were far too dangerous to attempt to enter in such conditions. Despite the tremendous seas the *Cambria* was abeam of the Longships lighthouse by 21.00 but Capt. Livingstone, with excellent seamanship ran her well south before making his turn for the English Channel so that he could bring the massive seas right astern.

The gale had now backed to the south-west and had increased to full hurricane force but Capt. Livingstone decided not to seek shelter in Penzance. The *Cambria* was abeam of The Lizard at midnight and off Start Point at dawn when she ran into serious trouble. The sea was covered with pit props; the deck cargo washed from a Norwegian ship during the night. One of the pit props fouled the starboard paddle wheel and had to be cut free with axes – a highly dangerous operation in which several members of the crew had to go through the paddle door in the engine room alleyway and out on to the paddle itself; a most unenviable task in the heavy seas which was, however, successfully accomplished.

All seemed to be going well until the *Cambria* was off Portland, when she was pooped by a tremendous sea, 'as high as the funnel', said a passenger, which stove in a number of the saloon windows on the starboard quarter and washed a number of passengers over to port. A second huge sea immediately followed which then smashed in several windows on the port side, a number of passengers being cut by flying plate glass. To quote the *South Wales Daily News* again;

> ...the tenants of the saloon were knee deep in water and each second would seem to decide the fate of the boat. A huge wave swept over the deck and carried two men swiftly to the side. A guy rope fortunately stayed their progress, otherwise their recovery from the sea would have been impossible.

During the storm Capt. Alec, extremely anxious for the *Cambria's* safety, paced the floor of his office all night and into the following day and was relieved when the Southampton agent telephoned him mid-morning on Tuesday 2 September to say that he could see her coming up Southampton Water. She docked at 12.00 a remarkable performance considering the extreme conditions. The newspaper report ends by stating:

Almost every passenger was drenched to the skin and as only a few had a change of clothing the position was a most trying one. Great credit is due to Capt. Livingstone for his clever handling of the boat and a hearty response was given by the disembarking passengers at Southampton to the call for three cheers for the captain.

By remarkably good fortune, one of the *Cambria*'s passengers had his camera with him and left to posterity an outstanding series of photographs, which are reproduced here. The photographer was Mr S.G. Chrimes, a seasoned excursion steamer traveller who had come from the South Coast to make the trip home by sea. When one considers that his equipment was not an easily portable miniature camera of today but a large and cumbersome plate camera using quarter-plate glass negatives, probably placed on a tripod, and that keeping one's feet was virtually impossible, the production of such photographs was an extraordinary achievement.

The severity of the storm, which ravaged the southern half of the country, can be gauged from the front page newspaper reports of the shipping casualties and also the extensive damage ashore. Some of the headlines from the *South Wales Daily News* of Wednesday 2 September 1908 stated:

SAILING SHIP WRECKED ON MARGAM SANDS. TWENTY LIVES LOST.

This referred to the four-masted barque *Amazon* which parted her cables in Swansea Bay and drove ashore to the east of Port Talbot where she broke in half. Of her complement of thirty there were only eight survivors; twenty-two were drowned within sight of the spectators ashore. The Mumbles lifeboat made gallant attempts to reach her but was defeated and the rockets fired by the shore crew were blown back by the force of the wind.

HELWICK LIGHTVESSEL BADLY DAMAGED

The lightvessel, in its exposed position off the Gower coast, was badly damaged by heavy seas and broke adrift. The Tenby lifeboat ran up channel before the wind and took off the crew. The Swansea pilot cutter *Beaufort* then towed the lifeboat into port.

THREE-MASTED SHIP *VERAJEAN* ASHORE AT RHOOSE

This full rigged ship, which had sailed from Cardiff two days before, was unable to make any progress against the wind and was eventually blown back up channel.

ABOARD THE *CAMBRIA* ON THE ROUND TRIP FROM BRISTOL TO
SOUTHAMPTON DURING THE SEVERE GALE OF TUESDAY 1 SEPTEMBER 1908.

This page and following page: *Running before the wind in Lyme Bay.*

Off Start Point, surrounded by pit props.

Engines stopped while a pit prop is cleared from the starboard paddle.

Slowly getting under way again. Captain Livingstone keeps a close eye on the ship's progress. Chief Officer Fred Nunn stands by on the port telegraph.

Full speed again.

A damaged lifebelt locker and seat.

In calmer conditions, steaming up Southampton Water.

Above and below: *Aboard the* Cambria *off the Isle of Wight on the afternoon of Tuesday 1 September 1908. Curtains, carpets and deck chairs are drying in the sun. Broken deck seats and lifebelt lockers have been put ashore for repair, and her funnel has already been repainted.*

The deck crew of the Cambria, *Tuesday 1 September 1908.*

The Cambria's *Purser, Mr Skinner, on the bridge, Tuesday 1 September 1908.*

Chief Engineer, Robert Wilson, on the bridge of the Cambria *on Tuesday 1 September 1908. The previous twenty-four hours had been particularly trying for him as he nursed and cajoled his vessel's engines through one of the worst storms in living memory.*

Of the *Cambria's* plight the headlines read:

CAMBRIA – EXCURSIONISTS PERIL
CAMBRIA HAS A ROUGH TIME
Passengers injured. Decks swept by giant waves.
Memorable trip from Cardiff.
Nearly a disaster.
Passed Lizard at midnight.

Ships were in trouble all along the South Coast. The cross-channel turbine steamer *Empress* spent three hours attempting to enter Folkestone Harbour but had to give up and divert to Dover: the Southampton Co.'s paddle steamer *Queen* ran aground at Selsey, and the *Balmoral* was storm-bound in Cherbourg for forty-eight hours, her captain having turned back to the French port after attempting to cross to Southampton.

In the Bristol Channel the *Brighton* had a very bad passage from Ilfracombe to Swansea on the evening of 31 August and was cancelled on the following day as were all Bristol Channel and south coast excursion steamers.

The Cambria *arriving at Brighton in September 1908.*

The Cambria *leaving Eastbourne in September 1908.*

Repairs to the *Cambria* were quickly carried out, so quickly in fact that she made her first trip, from Brighton to Eastbourne, Hastings and Folkestone on Wednesday 2 September. She visited Boulogne on the following day and on 9 and 12 September, as well as sailing regularly to Folkestone, Southampton and Ryde. Naturally, she did a great deal of running to and from Hastings in direct competition with the *Lady Rowena*.

The Cambria *at Ilfracombe on 10 October 1908, when the presentation of an Illuminated Address was made to Capt. Livingstone on behalf of the passengers who had been aboard during the severe gale.*

The *Cambria* did not succeed in 'running off' her competitor but her visit to Sussex, (which was never to be repeated), was nevertheless a great success; passenger figures on the whole being very high. The *Lady Rowena* continued her south coast services for Richard Collard until the end of the 1911 season, when she was sold to A.W. Cameron for service on the Clyde. During the intervening years, however, there appeared to be sufficient patronage to keep both Collard and the Campbells satisfied.

The *Cambria* returned to Bristol on 28 September 1908, but her season was not yet over. A fine spell of weather kept her on the Bristol–Cardiff–Ilfracombe run until 10 October, on which date the presentation of a framed illuminated address was made to Capt. Livingstone as the steamer lay at Ilfracombe Pier. This was made by those passengers who had been aboard on the round trip on 31 August, as a token of their gratitude and admiration. It was a fitting tribute to a master who had taken them through horrific conditions by way of his skill, seamanship, an element of sportsmanship and a generous helping of sheer daring!

1909

During the winter of 1908/1909 the *Cambria* went into Stothert's yard at Bristol, where her large saloon windows were removed and replaced by portholes. Curiously, the four large windows at the after end of the saloon, overlooking the quarter deck, remained for the rest of her career.

Cambria *and* Gwalia *at Ilfracombe, Easter 1909.*

Ravenswood *in the Cumberland Basin after being re-boilered and re-engined at Barclay & Curle's yard, Glasgow, 15 May 1909.*

The *Ravenswood* underwent considerable alterations during that winter. Alec had reported to the directors, in the autumn of 1908, that she was in need of new boilers and suggested that she should be fitted with compound engines which would make her a much more economical vessel. He estimated that the work would cost about £6,000 and was authorised to obtain tenders.

On 13 March 1909 the *Ravenswood* left Bristol, coaled at Cardiff, and arrived at Barclay & Curle's yard at Glasgow on 16 March. Capt. Henry Chidgey was in command, accompanied by Peter and Alec.

Her two haystack boilers were replaced by a single ended marine boiler with Howden's modified forced draught, working at a pressure of 125lb per square inch, a little more than double the pressure of the old boilers. Her new compound cylinders were 25.5in and 50in in diameter with a 54in stroke. Her coal consumption was halved with the loss of only half a knot in speed.

She left the Queens Dock, Glasgow, on 13 May and arrived back in Bristol two days later. Her appearance was quite transformed and much improved with her single funnel placed forward of the bridge.

The Barry Railway did not obtain the full running powers which they had sought in their Bill of February 1908, neither from the point of view of the railways nor the piers. The owners of the Birnbeck and Grand Piers at Weston, of Minehead and Ilfracombe flatly refused to entertain any investment by the company, for none of them wished to be 'under the thumb' of the Barry Railway. In the face of such opposition the company dropped the scheme. At the half-yearly shareholders meeting on 5 February 1909 there was, yet again, much opposition to the running of the steamers but the chairman stated that as they had only one year's experience of running the boats within the prescribed limits they had called in a 'competent expert' to advise them. He had made valuable suggestions with a view to making the boat service profitable and they felt that another year's trial should be carried out.

Possibly the 'competent expert', (who was not named), had thoughts of attempting to increase the speed of the *Devonia* and *Gwalia* for on 16 February 1909 John Brown & Co. submitted two tenders to the Barry Railway. One was for modifications to their existing paddles and the other was for completely new wheels; neither tender was accepted.

Both P&A Campbell Ltd and the Red Funnel Line began their seasons on Maundy Thursday 8 April 1909. The new low water pier at Weston was opened, unofficially, on 1 May 1909 but not officially until Whitsun as the roller skating rink had not been completed. The landing stage was 70ft from base to top deck to allow for the great rise and fall of the tide. It was claimed that there were 15ft of water at low tide but in reality there were only 6ft at low water springs. Exposed to SW and W winds it was not a success; the masters disliked it owing to the danger of over running the landing stage and grounding on the rocks of Birnbeck Island. Neither the P&A Campbell nor the Barry ships made calls at the Grand Pier this season.

Birnbeck Island in the spring of 1909, showing the low water pier, on the left, nearing completion.

Albion *and* Gwalia *at anchor off Clovelly in 1909.*

Brighton *and* Gwalia at Ilfracombe, 1907/1909.

On 7 July 1909 the *Western Mail* announced:

BARRY PLEASURE STEAMERS
PROPOSED SERVICE FROM SWANSEA.
The Barry Railway Company are taking steps to secure a berth at Swansea for the accommodation of one of their passenger steamers with a view to running a regular summer service between Swansea and Devonshire....

The boats will not enter the docks at Swansea but will use the Mumbles Pier and cheap fares have been arranged to and from Swansea on the Mumbles Railway.

The Swansea newspapers carried similar information but added that terms had not yet been agreed with the Swansea Harbour Trustees. In the event of an agreement, it was intended that the Red Funnel ships should use the *Normandy*'s old berth.

The *Normandy*, laid up since 1907, sailed from Swansea for Liverpool on 4 May 1909. She had been seized by her first mortgagee, the notorious Joseph Constant, who, true to form, sold her for scrap on arrival.

It was obvious that the Swansea Harbour Trustees wanted to keep the Barry steamers out; they had no intention of allowing them to 'run off' the *Brighton*, and consequently still insisted on a charge of £5 each time one of their steamers entered.

The *Barry* ran the only trip from Swansea in 1909, on 17 July, to Weston, advertised as 'The Trip of the Season'. Incidentally, on the same day, the *Gwalia*, bound from Barry to Mumbles to run a day trip to Ilfracombe, broke down off Porthcawl and had to return to Barry. For the rest of the season all Red Funnel trips were made from Mumbles Pier. The adverts ran:

Gwalia *arriving at Ilfracombe, 1907/1909.*

BARRY RAILWAY.
RED FUNNEL STEAMERS – *GWALIA, DEVONIA, BARRY.*
Combined Rail and Sea Excursions from Swansea (via Mumbles Pier).
The Quickest Route to Ilfracombe. Average Passage 1 hour 15 minutes.
Express Train from Rutland Street.

The last statement was rather comical. The old Mumbles steam train had a top speed of 20mph (and that only at very few places on the line); the 5½ mile journey to Mumbles Pier took twenty-five minutes.

The Barry steamers sailings from Mumbles took place every day, (except Sundays), throughout the season. There were day trips to Ilfracombe only, Ilfracombe and on to Lynmouth or Clovelly, and, unusually, trips to Lynmouth direct and Clovelly direct. There were day and afternoon trips to Porthcawl, and afternoon and evening trips along the Gower Coast; in short, a very intensive programme. The ships bunkered at Barry and came back to Mumbles next morning but on the nights they did not need bunkering they anchored off Mumbles.

The *Brighton* did not appear to be unduly worried by the competition of the Red Funnel steamers. The latter charged 3s day return to Ilfracombe, including second class rail fare on the Mumbles train, pier tolls at Mumbles and saloon accommodation on the steamer. From Mumbles Pier only the fare was 2s9d. The *Brighton* replied by charging only 1s for an afternoon trip to Ilfracombe on Thursdays, (early closing day in Swansea), and Saturdays.

Barry *and* Gwalia *at Barry, 1908/1909.*

Devonia *and* Westonia *at Barry.*

Above and below: Cambria *arriving at Porthcawl, 1909/1911*.

Passengers aboard the Albion *at Ilfracombe on 19 July 1909. Alongside is the* Westward Ho.

Bonnie Doon *in the Cumberland Basin, 1907/1912.*

An array of Edwardian finery. Passengers aboard the Gwalia *at Ilfracombe on 14 August 1909.*

The half-yearly meeting of the Barry Railway shareholders took place on 20 July 1909 when the chairman stated that the directors were closely watching the working of the steamers. A shareholder, Mr Thomas Morel, said that in spite of increased traffic the company had declared the lowest dividend in its history. In his opinion if the company continued with its steamer operations it would lead to a most serious situation. Another shareholder, Mr John Ferrier, also made a lengthy speech in which he highlighted the considerable depreciation which had been incurred and added:

> If anything was of any guide to the directors, as men of business, surely four years of experience in running the boats was quite sufficient to influence them in making a definite decision.

The chairman then stated that if the shareholders now said that they did not want to force the hands of the directors, he was quite willing to leave the ultimate decision to the shareholders themselves.

Nothing further was decided at the meeting but in the autumn of 1909 the directors very discreetly let it be known that they were open to offers for the purchase of the steamers. Not a word was leaked to the press and not the slightest hint was given to the shareholders.

The first to nibble at the bait was the Furness Railway. Unfortunately, most of the correspondence of the Furness Railway has not been preserved but from the surviving letters of the Barry Railway in the Public Records Office at Kew it seems that the Furness Railway made an offer for the *Devonia* in early November 1909.

The general manager of the Barry Railway sent a copy of a letter from the Furness Railway's general manager, Mr A.A. Aslett, to the directors together with a copy of his reply. The Furness Railway letter was dated 23 December 1909 and stated:

I acknowledge receipt of your letter of 20 December but entirely dissent from your suggestion that the Furness Co. can be called upon to purchase the *Devonia*, and that there is any contract which they can be required to complete.

There never was a concluded bargain. If you agreed the price at £22,000 it was still subject to this company being satisfied with the result of an inspection.

The Furness Railway never agreed to be satisfied with an inspection afloat but, on the contrary, insisted on the vessel being dry docked and opened up. The deposit, as you were aware, was made several days before you offered to agree the price. It was made quite clear throughout that my directors would not bind themselves to buy the vessel until they were satisfied with the results of the inspection. They were not satisfied and therefore refused to give the confirmation which you invited by your telegram of 8 December. As the sale has fallen through I am prepared, without admitting that there is a legal liability in respect of such expenses, to advise my board to allow you a fair and reasonable sum in respect of the cost of dry docking this vessel for our inspection, but subject to this I must repeat the request that you return the deposit without further delay.

The Barry company's reply was dated 30 December 1909:

Adverting to your letter dated 23 December, your company made a positive offer for this steamer as she then stood and pressed my company to accept the offer after the inspection was completed, which we did. I would point out to you that the ship was not sold to your company as a new steamer, but was a second-hand boat, and so far we have not received from you any particulars of any fault in the steamer, notwithstanding our request to be furnished with the information.

The meeting of the steamboat committee on 7 December was required to come to a decision as to the acceptance of the Furness Railway's offer of £22,000 for the *Devonia*. A series of telegrams had passed during the day between the companies and a definite reply was pressed for submission to a meeting of our directors on the following day. At that meeting it was decided to send the following telegram – 'Committee accept your offer of £22,000 on assumption that you inspection is satisfactory and subject to confirmation tomorrow'.

The Furness Railway, however, refused to move. The news eventually reached the newspapers and during February 1910 letters appeared in the *Western Mail* from various shareholders with pointed questions about the Barry steamers:

..Are we going to be relieved of the expensive folly of running steamers any longer?

...To continue the steamers under present conditions in the face of a reasonable offer would be unpardonable policy...

It is known that Mr John Conacher had been called in as a consultant, possibly he was the 'competent expert' referred to at the meeting of 5 February 1909. He had been chairman and managing director of the Cambrian Railway and had been with the North British Railway prior to that. He was appointed general manager of the Barry Railway on 10 February 1910 at the then 'fabulous' salary of £1,000 per year.

At the half-yearly shareholders meeting on 10 February 1910 Mr T. Morel stated that the loss on the steamers was now £15,000 per annum and he moved that every endeavour should be made to dispose of them at a fair market price. Mr J. Ferrier said that as long as the steamers ran from Barry it was physically impossible to fill them. He believed the steamers would earn a living and a dividend for any adventurer who would run them from other ports of the Bristol Channel as well as Barry. The chairman stated that the directors had adopted the policy of endeavouring in the best possible way to dispose of the steamers.

The Furness Railway again sent representatives to Barry on 28 February 1910, this time to inspect the *Gwalia*. John Conacher wired to A.A. Aslett at Barrow on 18 March, 'Cannot accept offer of £20,000 but if you will increase your offer to £22,500 we are prepared to consider and give a prompt reply'. Mr Aslett's reply is unknown but John Conacher wired him again on 1 April, 'We will sell *Gwalia* for £22,500 if approved by you afloat. Contract for purchase must then be signed and deposit paid. Contract will provide dry docking and reasonable opening out at cost of purchaser'.

The Furness Railway accepted and paid a deposit of £2,175 on 27 April 1910 but it was not until 3 May that the *Gwalia* went into the Barry Graving Dock for inspection. The defects found were, 'No.2 and No.3 keel plates badly dented. No.7 plate portside indented. Rudder worn down and pintle slack'. The defects were made good and she came out of the graving dock on the following day. The Bill of Sale was dated 7 May 1910.

Capt. Thomas of the Furness Railway, brought a crew to Barry and the *Gwalia* sailed at 11.00 on 10 May, arriving at Ramsden Dock, Barrow, at 04.00 on the following day – a fast run. Her funnels were immediately painted buff but her hull was left black for the rest of the season. Her first trip, still as the *Gwalia*, was from Barrow to Fleetwood on Saturday 14 May. It was not until Saturday 11 June 1910 that she ran under her new name of *Lady Moyra*; so named after Lady Moyra Cavendish, wife of Lord Richard Cavendish, a director of the Furness Railway and brother of the Duke of Devonshire.

The Barry Railway made desperate efforts to dispose of the remaining three steamers. The *Western Mail* reported, on 14 April 1910:

Above and below: Gwalia *at Barrow in Furness. May 1910.*

A strong local syndicate has been formed for the purpose of acquiring the Barry Railway passenger steamers. Negotiations have been in progress for some weeks past between the company and a syndicate of influential business men in Cardiff.

A week later the syndicate members were named as:

Mr John Best Ferrier – Chairman – *a director of Burnyeat, Brown & Co., of Cardiff, Coal exporters.*
Mr Thomas Edward Morel – *one of the leading shipowners in Cardiff.*

These two gentlemen had had been the most persistent and violent critics of the Barry Railway's handling of its steamer business.
Mr John Cory – *of John Cory & Sons, a shipowner and chairman of the Cardiff Channel Dry Docks & Pontoon Co. Ltd.*
Mr Hilary Blondel Marquand – *of Martin & Marquand, tug owners. A director of Hills Dry Dock & Engineering Co. Ltd.*
Mr Humphrey Wallis – *of Osborne & Wallis. A shipowner and director of the Great Western Colliery Co. Ltd. and also Lockett's Merthyr Collieries.*
Mr David Percival Barnett – *of F.H. Lambert, Barnett & Co. A shipowner.*

Prior to the complete formation of the syndicate, and in order to dispose of the steamers as quickly as possible, the Barry Railway wrote, on 2 May 1910, to Joseph Davies, of Davies and Hailey, coal exporters, (two of the original backers of the formation of the Barry Railway), offering the *Devonia, Barry* and *Westonia* for £42,000. The offer was apparently excessive, but after negotiations, on 12 May 1910 the Barry Railway sold the steamers to Joseph Davies and Claud Hailey for £39,000.

The syndicate styled itself 'The Bristol Channel Passenger Boats Ltd'; the capital being £70,000 in £1 shares for which applications closed on 27 May. The steamers began sailing from Cardiff on 14 May, still owned by Davies and Hailey, and still in the old Barry Railway colours. It was not until 16 June 1910 that the Bill of Sale was made out to Bristol Channel Passenger Boats Ltd, the latter buying them from Davies and Hailey for £39,500.

The Barry Railway's venture into the excursion steamer business had been an extremely costly mistake which ended in ignominious defeat. The company never again exercised its powers to run passenger steamers under the 1904 Act.

'We don't get summers like we used to'

1910

The old adage 'We don't get summers like we used to' is often heard but the records show that the summers of 'years ago' were often as bad as those of the present. The halcyon summer of 1911 for example was preceded by the 'shocker' of 1910. The season was very wet and stormy, particularly at the end of June and in August. Nevertheless, passages were consistently made down channel in very heavy seas.

In spite of the bad weather, traffic on the Cardiff to Weston ferry steadily increased, especially at the height of the season, from mid-July to the end of August. The *Waverley* and *Ravenswood* were employed almost exclusively on this route and often had to be backed up by the *Albion* at the expense of the Newport station.

Bristol Channel Passenger Boats Ltd advertised itself as the Red Funnel Line and, like P&A Campbell Ltd, began running at Easter 1910. Their steamers bunkered at Barry, lay there overnight and left light, early in the morning for Cardiff to carry out their day's sailings. The *Westonia* and *Barry* were also mainly employed on the ferry, occasionally having to be augmented by the *Devonia*.

The upsurge in ferry traffic was a cause of particular concern to Capt. Alec. On 20 June he left Bristol for Barrow-in-Furness to make arrangements for chartering the Furness Railway's paddle steamer *Philomel*, which, he hoped, would ease the situation. The *Philomel* had been purchased from the General Steam Navigation Co. of London after the Furness Railway's former White Funnel steamer, *Lady Margaret*, had been sold to the Admiralty in March 1908 for use as a tender. On the arrival of the *Gwalia* in May 1910 the *Philomel* was laid up in Barrow.

A charter was agreed and a payment of £500 was made as the first instalment but when Alec arrived in Barrow, together with a crew for the voyage south, he found that her boiler was leaking so badly that he refused to accept delivery. The Furness Railway declined to cancel the charter so Alec placed the matter before his solicitors. On 5 September Alec reported to the board that a cheque for £550 had been received from the Furness Railway, which he, and the board, considered to be a satisfactory settlement of the matter.

Brighton Queen *(left), and* Ravenswood *at Bristol early in 1910. A cowl top has now been fitted to the funnel of the* Ravenswood.

Ravenswood *at Bristol early in 1910.*

'WISH YOU WERE HERE'? A SELECTION OF POSTCARDS TAKEN BY THE ILFRACOMBE PHOTOGRAPHERS DURING THE GALES OF 1910, AND SOLD THROUGHOUT THE TOWN.

Above and below: Britannia *passing Rillage Point on her approach to Ilfracombe Pier, 29 June 1910.*

Cambria *off to Clovelly, 29 June 1910.*

Brighton *arriving at Ilfracombe, 30 June 1910.*

Above and below: Devonia *making her way towards Ilfracombe, 30 June 1910.*

Ravenswood *off Penarth, 1910/1911.*

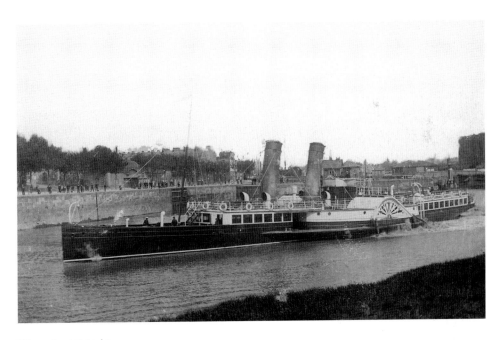

Westonia *at Bristol in 1910.*

Albion *arriving at Ilfracombe in the 1900s.*

Bonnie Doon *at Newport, 1910.*

Barry at Bristol *1908/1910.*

Devonia *in the river Avon, 1910/1911.*

Barry off Ilfracombe in the 1900s.

The only P&A Campbell memorandum book to have survived from the pre-First World War years is that of 1910, and some extracts from it will perhaps be of interest despite their somewhat terse and jerky style:

Saturday 14 May
Devonia arrived at Weston from Barry. Had no passengers, embarked 10 for Cardiff, Minehead and Ilfracombe....
Ravenswood took 856 passengers from Cardiff & Penarth to Clevedon & Bristol...

Monday 23 May
Brighton Queen. Brighton to Cherbourg, left Palace Pier 09.00 with 400 passengers. Arrived Cherbourg 14.25.
Saturday 28 May
Cambria left Cardiff five minutes astern of *Westonia*, called at Penarth and passed her about half way across. *Westonia* did not call at Penarth. *Cambria* 24 minutes from Penarth to Honeycomb Buoy.

Wednesday 1 June
Albion. Cardiff, Penarth, Minehead, Lynmouth, Ilfracombe & Clovelly. Capt. Webber states *Albion* left Lynmouth 4 or 5 lengths ahead of *Devonia*. Abreast off Rillage but *Albion* had inside berth. *Albion* arrived Ilfracombe 12.42 but *Devonia* had to lie off and berthed at 12.55.

Saturday 11 June
Ravenswood, to Penarth and Mumbles 06.30. Mumbles to Swansea light. Chartered as Committee Boat for Swansea Bay Regatta.

Tuesday 14 June
Cambria at Lynmouth 12 minutes. Landed between 20 and 30, took on 50. One Lynmouth passenger fell into water while embarking. Boatmen took him back to shore before coming out again to *Cambria*.

Thursday 16 June
Cambria beat *Devonia* into Ilfracombe by 5 minutes.

Wednesday 29 June
Wind SW strong to gale. *Cambria* went on to Clovelly. (See page 187).

Thursday 30 June
Blowing hard from NW. Heavy sea in channel. No landing at Lynmouth. *Cambria* had five portholes smashed or cracked in sponson houses. *Britannia* had wooden panel split in forward companionway, seats damaged.

A rather 'scruffy' Devonia *arriving at Ilfracombe on 14 July 1910.*

Tuesday 23 August
Britannia left Bristol 5 minutes behind *Devonia*. Passed her off Portishead and arrived at Ilfracombe 19 minutes ahead.

Wednesday 24 August
Wind westerly, fresh. *Britannia* broke three windows in heavy seas off Minehead. Young lady passenger had head cut open. Taken to doctor in Minehead – severed artery in temple – sent home by rail.

Sea going over breakwater at Porthcawl. Understand good many passengers would not board *Cambria*. Ship swilling with water from stem to stern on departure.

Friday 26 August
Blowing hard from west. *Britannia* for Clevedon, Weston, Mumbles and Tenby, but did not go on to Tenby. Sea stove in chartroom panel and carried away teak rail forward. Returned from Mumbles at 18.20 and did not call at Clevedon.

The rivalry between Bristol Channel Passenger Boats and P&A Campbell Ltd, although keen, never reached the intensity of the Edwards, Robertson days of the 1890s. The memorandum book, however, records with monotonous regularity the timings of the 'races' between the *Devonia* and the *Cambria* and *Britannia,* most of which were won by the White Funnel steamers. This was hardly surprising as the latter were kept in such excellent condition, whereas the Red Funnel ships became sadly lacking in the matter of upkeep both cosmetically and mechanically. However, Capt. Livingstone, of the *Cambria,* reported that on Monday 12 September 1910 his ship was beaten by the *Devonia*. He added that the latter was steaming 'dead light' and he had heard that the company had cleaned all her boiler tubes and bored the salt out; the inference here being that salt water had been used in the boilers. The *Cambria's* mate, Frederick Nunn, stated that he had heard that they had cleaned out no less than 150 tubes, and added that the *Devonia* passed the *Cambria* 'fair and square' after a good run, going in front of her as they were approaching Clovelly.

Other references in the memorandum book mention the fact that the three Red Funnel ships were looking very dirty; a complete contrast from their earlier years. Whatever one may think about the Barry Railway's exploits it must be allowed that under their ownership the vessels were kept in excellent condition.

The *Devonia* ended her season on about 23 September 1910, leaving the *Barry* to carry out the remaining Ilfracombe trips until these ceased on 1 October. The final White Funnel sailing down channel, later than usual, was performed by the *Westward Ho* when she took 341 passengers from Bristol to Clevedon, Cardiff, Penarth, Lynmouth and Ilfracombe on Monday 10 October 1910.

Capt. Alec was determined to secure a new steamer to ease the pressure on the ferry during the following season and requested quotations from a variety of

Above and below: Britannia, *now with a cowl top on her funnel, leaving Bristol, 1910/1911.*

A view from Penarth Head of Capt. Robert Falcon Scott's Terra Nova *leaving Cardiff, bound for Antarctica. 15 June 1910. The* Devonia *and* Ravenswood *were in attendance and escorted her to off Barry.*

Ravenswood *and* Terra Nova *off Penarth. 15 June 1910.*

Ravenswood *and* Terra Nova *off Penarth. 15 June 1910.*

Brighton Queen *leaving Ryde, 1910.*

Brighton Queen *at Dover in the 1900s.*

Clyde shipbuilders, the lowest of which was £16,820 from the Ailsa Co. of Troon. This was an extraordinarily low figure but the Ailsa Co. were no doubt thinking of future orders. Incidentally, the Ailsa Co. had taken over McKnight's yard at Ayr in February 1902, both yards now being run in conjunction as the Ailsa Shipbuilding & Engineering Co. Ltd of Troon and Ayr. Alec reported on 13 December 1910 that the order for the new steamer had been placed with the Ailsa Co. and that Peter had journeyed north to go into the necessary details concerning her design.

1911

In 1911 P&A Campbell Ltd embarked on a policy of modifying and improving the older members of the fleet. Early in the year the *Waverley* went into Stothert's yard at Bristol for alterations. The large saloon windows, except those right aft, were plated in with portholes, and her bridge was moved forward of the funnel which received a cowl top with a pronounced slope. She left Bristol on 8 April 1911 for Southampton, then on to Brighton, running from there from Easter until the *Glen Rosa* arrived at Whitsun. The *Waverley* then became the Hastings boat in place of the *Bonnie Doon*. The latter remained in the Bristol Channel and became the 'odd job' steamer, helping the *Albion* at Newport, assisting on the ferry and occasionally acting as a tender to the Royal Line ships at Avonmouth, landing their passengers and baggage when the liners were unable to enter the locks until the tide served.

The *Glen Rosa* ran in the Bristol Channel at Easter 1911 in her original P&A Campbell guise but was then taken in hand for modifications. Her raised quarterdeck

Left to right: Bonnie Doon, Waverley *and* Glen Rosa *in the Merchant's Dock, Bristol, in the spring of 1911.*

Albion *at Newport in the 1900s.*

Waverley *in the Cumberland Basin on 8 April 1911. She is about to leave Bristol for the South Coast.*

Aboard Waverley *on her first trip of the season from Brighton, Wednesday 12 April 1911.*

Glen Rosa *off Brighton, 1911.*

Capt. David James with the officers and crew of the Glen Rosa, *1911.*

Waverley *at Eastbourne Pier, 1911.*

The lack of holidaymakers indicates that it is tea time at Ventnor on a tranquil Saturday afternoon in 1911. The Waverley *waits at the pier for her evening return to Brighton, Eastbourne and Hastings.*

was removed and a saloon was constructed aft with the deck continuous with that existing around the bridge and funnel. Her topsides were plated in with ports and a dining saloon was added below the main saloon. Her bridge was moved forward of the funnel but for some reason a cowl top was not fitted until the following winter. The *Glen Rosa* sailed from Bristol on 31 May 1911 for Southampton and Brighton in readiness to begin her season.

At the board meeting on 3 April 1911 the secretary read a letter from the Ailsa Co. which stated that they undertook to deliver the new steamer by 31 May, on payment of an additional sum of £350 for the necessary overtime which was agreed. The builders, however, failed to meet this deadline. The much delayed launch was to have taken place on 20 May but this was postponed until 27 May and even then again postponed.

The vessel was designed for economy in running combined with great passenger carrying capacity. She was 220ft long, (between perpendiculars), by 26ft beam and just over 8ft depth. She was, therefore, shorter by 5ft that the *Westward Ho* and *Cambria*, and of shallower draught for operating at Cardiff. There were to be no pretensions to speed, the *Britannia* and *Cambria* could deal effectively with any opposition that might arise. The engines being built by the Ailsa Co. had small cylinders, only 26.5in by 52in with a stroke of 54in. Her boiler was also small measuring 15.5ft in diameter by 11.5in in length – a single ended marine type with only three furnaces, working at a pressure of 125lb per square inch, with Howden's modified forced draught.

Miss Nellie Campbell, (Helen Hunter Campbell – Capt. Peter's daughter), was to have performed the launching ceremony, she having gone to stay with her aunt, Mrs Hugh Highgate of Blairmore, (Peter and Alec's sister Isabella). Two days before the launch Nellie was taken ill with mumps. Mrs Highgate informed the Ailsa Co. and it was agreed that she should perform the ceremony in place of Nellie.

The launch took place on 1 June 1911, Mrs Highgate naming the steamer *Lady Ismay*, after Lady Ismay Crichton Stuart, wife of Lord Ninian Crichton Stuart, brother of the Marquis of Bute.

There were several unusual features for a Campbell steamer in the *Lady Ismay*: no windows this time but portholes throughout; the after companionway was covered by the reserved deckhouse, as in the *Gwalia*, *Devonia* and *Barry*. With the engine room being so much smaller, there was much more space between the engine room casing and the ship's sides, giving a great impression of roominess. The paddle wheels were much smaller – only 14ft 11.5in in diameter, with seven floats 10ft 1in by 3ft. The paddle shafts were set much lower so that passengers making their way along the main deck did not have to clamber up steps to cross the boxed-in shafts, as in the *Westward Ho*, *Cambria* and *Britannia*.

A profile of Lady Ismay Crichton Stuart formed the device at the centre of her paddle boxes which were extremely low in height. Two gangways forward and two abaft the paddle boxes could be used together with a double width gangway on the paddle box platform which enabled approximately 100 passengers per minute to be embarked or disembarked. She had one funnel with a flat cowl similar to that of the *Brighton Queen*, *Britannia* and *Westward Ho*.

Her specifications allowed her a No.2 certificate enabling her to ply anywhere in the United Kingdom or to the northern ports of France. This, however, was not the company's intention. She had been designed mainly with the ferry in mind and her No.4 certificate enabled her to carry 1,020 passengers on that service – 201 more than the *Ravenswood*, 317 more than the *Waverley*, 273 more than the *Albion*, and even 5 more than the *Devonia*!

Lady Ismay *fitting out at the Ailsa Shipbuilding Co.'s yard at Troon. June 1911.*

Ravenswood *ashore near Lavernock Point, 7 June 1911.*

Mavis *arriving at Ilfracombe, 1911/1913.*

Mavis *leaving Swansea, 1911/1913.*

Above and below: Brighton *leaving Swansea, 1911/1914.*

Cheaper than dry docking! Over the low water period, the Brighton *has been temporarily beached at Ilfracombe for cleaning and painting below the waterline, 1911/1914.*

While the *Lady Ismay's* fitting out progressed several interesting events occurred in the Bristol Channel. On the night of 6/7 June the *Ravenswood* lay at anchor in Cardiff Roads, owing to the Pier Head berths being full. Her anchor dragged and she was found to be high and dry on the following morning on the beach near Lavernock. Luckily she had chosen to rest on a flat bed of sand and mud and floated off undamaged on the following high tide.

Pockett's Bristol Channel Steam Packet Co. brought the former General Steam Navigation Co.'s paddle steamer *Mavis* into service at the beginning of June 1911 but she offered little competition to P&A Campbell Ltd, being mainly employed on the Swansea to Ilfracombe service with occasional visits to Clovelly. The *Mavis*, incidentally, was a sister ship of the Furness Railway's *Philomel*, previously mentioned in connection with the abortive charter of 1910.

On Saturday 24 June 1911 King George V's Coronation Naval Review took place in Spithead and the *Britannia*, *Westward Ho* and *Devonia* were sent around for the occasion.

The *Westward Ho* left Bristol on Thursday 22 June at 15.50 calling at Clevedon, Cardiff, Penarth and leaving Ilfracombe at 20.15 for Bournemouth. On the following afternoon she made a cruise around the assembled fleet and on Saturday 24 June made a further cruise through the lines of warships before anchoring for the Review itself. She returned from Bournemouth at 06.00 on the Sunday and was due at Bristol at 03.30 on Monday 26 June.

Westward Ho at the Royal Naval Review in Spithead, Saturday 24 June 1911. The bow of the Brighton Queen *can be seen on the left.*

The *Britannia* appears to have been on charter; no adverts appeared for any round trip from either Bristol or Cardiff outwards, but she was advertised for the return trip direct to Bristol. She did not leave Bournemouth until 08.15 on Monday 26 June and was due in Bristol at 03.30 on the following day.

One of the few surviving log books from the pre-1914 era is that of the *Devonia* for 1911. It shows that on Thursday 22 June, after running a day trip to Ilfracombe, she returned to Barry to take on coal before leaving again at 20.40. She then left Ilfracombe at 23.22, passed Trevose Head at 03.20 on 23 June, the Longships at 08.00, Start Point at 11.10 and arrived at Southampton at 17.05. On Saturday 24 June she ran a cruise to Spithead at 12.30, returned and departed at 16.15 for the Review, arriving back in Southampton at 23.55. After making two cruises around the fleet on the Sunday she sailed for Cardiff at 21.00. She reached Ilfracombe at 15.00 on Monday 26 June, departed at 16.05 and arrived in Cardiff at 21.00.

The three south coast steamers, *Brighton Queen*, *Waverley* and *Glen Rosa* were also at the Review.

With her fitting out complete, the *Lady Ismay* ran her trials at Skelmorlie on Wednesday 5 July 1911 in a southerly gale. As a consequence, her best mean speed was only 15.55 knots but she was well capable of a good 17 knots under better conditions. The gale also meant that none of the official photographers could put out in their small boats so no photographs were taken of the occasion.

The wind had moderated by that evening and she left Troon at 20.00 under the command of Capt. Peter Campbell. Dan Taylor would normally have brought her south but he had now replaced Peter in command of the *Britannia* and as

Devonia on a cruise through the lines of warships at the Royal Naval Review in Spithead, June 1911.

Commodore of the fleet. Peter had retired from the bridge at the end of the 1910 season and had since taken a place on the board as a director.

Thick fog encountered in the St George's Channel delayed the *Lady Ismay*'s delivery voyage and she anchored in Penarth Roads at just after 18.00 on Thursday 6 July. There she waited for the tide and docked at Bristol in the early hours of the following day. She moored in the floating harbour alongside Hotwells Road where she was thrown open for public inspection during the day. After bunkering that night, she left for Cardiff on the early morning tide of 8 July; Capt. Henry Chidgey, his officers and crew having been transferred *en bloc* from the *Ravenswood* into the new ship.

The *Lady Ismay*'s maiden trip was from Cardiff to Weston at 08.15 that day. The *Devonia* was also put on the same run at 08.15 to 'show her up' in the matter of speed and was thought easily capable of giving her the 'go by'. The Cardiff passengers at the Pier Head made a rush for the new steamer – all 800 of them – leaving only a handful for the *Devonia*. Capt. Chidgey, continually checking his watch, let go precisely at 08.15 and heaved his ship around the dolphin-head with the stern rope to prevent the *Devonia* from backing out. When the ship's head had canted sufficiently he slammed the engine room telegraph to 'Full ahead', completely disregarding the warning notice board 'Speed 8 miles an Hour' and went tearing down the Cardiff drain. She called at Penarth, using only a spring fore and aft, hurried her passengers aboard and set off for Weston as fast as he could go. The *Devonia* did not call at Penarth as the *Lady Ismay* had scooped up all the passengers, but it was not until the latter had past the Honeycomb Buoy, off Weston, that the *Devonia* overhauled her and took the pier first. It was, nevertheless, a valiant attempt.

The *Lady Ismay* made her first trip down channel on Monday 17 July 1911, leaving Cardiff at 07.45 and sailing direct to Bristol. She then left Hotwells at 10.00 and returned to Cardiff in time to leave the Pier Head at 12 noon for Ilfracombe where she arrived, dressed overall, in beautiful weather, at 14.25.

Although confined mainly to the ferry the *Lady Ismay* made several trips to Ilfracombe, occasionally going on to Clovelly, and a favourite trip from Cardiff, advertised as by 'The New Saloon Steamer – *Lady Ismay*', was to witness the arrivals and departures of the Royal Line's *Royal George* or *Royal Edward* at Avonmouth

Lady Ismay *arriving at Penarth in 1911.*

Britannia *(left), and* Cambria *backing out of Ilfracombe together after lying side by side at the face of the pier,* 29 August 1911.

Opposite above: Lady Ismay *arriving at Ilfracombe on her first visit to North Devon, Monday 17 July 1911.*

Opposite below: Lady Ismay *steaming down channel from Ilfracombe in 1911.*

Cambria *leaving Ilfracombe, 1909/1911.*

The Campbell brothers were delighted with their new ship but a problem arose during the course of the season. The summer of 1911 was remarkably fine with long spells of hot weather and record temperatures. As built, the *Lady Ismay* had no engine room ventilators and the engine room became unbearably hot. To solve the problem she was taken into the Underfall Yard in August when a ventilator was fitted on either side of the reserved deckhouse.

The Red Funnel steamers' seasons progressed well until the end of August. A few trips are worthy of note, one being the *Westonia's* trip to Ilfracombe on 5 June 1911 – it was a very rare occurrence for her to venture down channel, and the others being the *Devonia's* charter trips from Port Talbot to Ilfracombe on 13 and 27 July. On both occasions she left Barry at 05.00 for Port Talbot and returned to Barry each night. Both were extended to Clovelly and on 13 July she made a cruise from Clovelly to off Tintagel.

The *Devonia* experienced a serious breakdown on 1 September. She had left Cardiff, Penarth and Barry for Mumbles and Tenby with a cruise from Tenby towards the Elegug Stack Rocks. She had just turned off the Pembrokeshire coast to head back to Tenby when a sudden jolt was felt and the chief engineer reported that the low pressure crank pin had become heated. She returned to Tenby at half speed and on making a further examination the engineers found that the crank pin had broken and the engines could not be restarted. Arrangements were made with the GWR to send two special trains to take the passengers home and two tugs were sent for. The *Dauntless* and the *Lady Morgan* duly arrived but while towing the *Devonia* from Tenby at 06.00 on the following day her stern fell heavily against the pier, damaging the stern boat and bending its davits. It was not until 19.00 that evening that the *Devonia* arrived at Barry. She was immediately withdrawn from service for the rest of the season, leaving the *Barry* to carry out the remaining down channel trips.

Britannia *in the river Avon, passing the village of Pill, on Regatta Day, 1910/1911.*

Devonia *disembarking passengers at Clovelly, 1911.*

Barry swinging at Tongue Head in 1911. Astern of her, about to enter the New Cut, (the section of the river Avon which was diverted prior to the building of the Floating Harbour), is the Cardiff to Bristol packet steamer The Marchioness.

The 1911 season had been a bumper one for P&A Campbell Ltd. The *Lady Ismay* had proved very popular with the public and Alec was pressing for another new steamer. As early as August he was asking for tenders. The Ailsa Co's records state:

8 August 1911
Enquiry from P. & A. Campbell Ltd. for a paddle steamer, repeat of the *Lady Ismay* with slight modifications, for delivery by 30 April 1912. Price £19,000.

Mr John Best Ferrier, chairman of Bristol Channel Passenger Boats, and mainspring of the company, died on 26 August 1911. His death, and the accident to the *Devonia* seemed to take the heart out of Bristol Channel Passenger Boats Ltd, for on 30 September 1911 Mr C.P. Hailey, of Davies & Hailey, the company which had negotiated the sale of the Barry steamers, approached Capt. Alec at his Cumberland Basin office and suggested an amalgamation of the two companies for the price of £45,000.

Alec reported Mr Hailey's visit to the board on 9 October and was authorised to make a counter offer of £30,000. Alec also stated that as the *Britannia* and *Cambria* would both require new boilers he had obtained prices from Dunsmuir & Jackson Ltd of Govan. As the prices mentioned were favourable, and to ensure early delivery he had accepted their offer of £2,260 and £2,150 respectively. The board approved.

The secretary then produced quotations from the Ailsa Co. and several other Clyde shipbuilders for a new steamer. Alec stated that the order should be placed immediately as no doubt the proposed amalgamation of the Red Funnel steamers would take several months to complete. It was then agreed that the order should be placed with the Ailsa Co. at the price quoted by them, (£19,000), for a duplicate of the *Lady Ismay*, but 1ft wider in beam.

In November 1911 Bristol Channel Passenger Boats Ltd. rejected P&A Campbell's offer of £30,000 but reduced their asking price to £35,000; Alec responded with an offer of £32,000 which again was rejected. Alec had received a report on the conditions of the steamers and met with the BCPB directors, after which he informed his board that in his opinion £34,000 was the lowest offer which would be entertained. After a long discussion it was resolved that the assets and undertaking of the Bristol Channel Passenger Boats should be purchased for £34,000.

The actual terms of the takeover were that £18,500 would be payable in cash and the remainder would be met by the issue of shares of 5s each, fully paid, in P&A Campbell Ltd. The shares would carry no final dividend as to 1911, but for future dividends they would be on exactly the same footing as the existing P&A Campbell ordinary shares.

A special meeting of BCPB Ltd was held in Cardiff on 4 December 1911 to agree the contract. The Bills of Sale of the steamers were dated 6 December 1911, and mortgages on the *Lady Ismay*, *Devonia* and *Barry* were taken out by P&A Campbell with Parr's Bank to raise the money for the purchase. The *Westonia* and the *Barry* were towed to Bristol on 14 and 17 December respectively, but the *Devonia* went to Avonmouth under her own steam on 19 December.

It has frequently been asserted that the Red Funnel ships received minimum alteration on their acquisition by P&A Campbell Ltd other than repainting and the addition of cowl tops to their funnels. This is certainly not correct.

There had always been a problem with passing the *Devonia* in and out of the locks of the Cumberland Basin owing to her great beam. P&A Campbell Ltd had a plan of the locks on which the width available was marked off at every six inches of water. The lock walls had a 'V' shaped cross section – the lower the water, the narrower the space between them.

The *Devonia* was to have her sponsons reduced in width, this meant that the star centre – an integral part of the paddle wheel feathering mechanism – would have to be shifted inboard and that consequently new paddles would have to be fitted. Mr W.J. Banks, in later years, claimed to have designed the new wheels but the late John MacGregor, Superintendent Engineer after Capt. Peter, said, 'No. Peter Campbell designed the wheels but Mr Banks produced the scantlings'. The work was to be carried out by A.&J. Inglis at Pointhouse, Glasgow.

The *Barry* had to have white lead pumped between the deck cover planks on the promenade deck and the stringer plates as rust was coming through. The engine room skylight was removed from the top of the forward end of the reserved deckhouse allowing the rails on top of the deckhouse to be extended further forward, thus gaining extra space. The wings of the reserved deckhouse had been removed by BCPB Ltd. Dated photographic evidence shows that they were there on 11 June 1911, but by early August they had disappeared.

The *Westonia* was taken in hand at Stothert's yard and was practically rebuilt. She was plated in with portholes; the forward sponson companionways were decked over and a new companionway was constructed amidships. She was not reboiled but the two uptakes were trunked into a single funnel fitted with a deep, cowl top with the bridge moved forward. The Barry Railway had replaced the fan shaped vents in the paddle box faces with concentric slats as in the other Red Funnel steamers, and these remained. New paddle wheels were built in the Underfall Yard and these were indeed designed by Mr W.J. Banks.

The work on the three steamers began at the end of the 1911 season and progressed well until early in 1912 when a particularly frustrating obstacle was encountered.

THE GOLDEN YEARS

1912

The great coal strike, when almost a million miners ceased work throughout the country, began on 12 February 1912, and seriously hampered P&A Campbell's refitting and reboilering programme. The company held good stocks of bunker coal but sold the greater part of it to the Royal Line at a very handsome profit. The Easter sailings, which began on Maundy Thursday 4 April, were consequently much curtailed. The *Bonnie Doon* and *Albion* maintained the Cardiff to Weston, Newport to Weston and Bristol to Cardiff trips, while the only Ilfracombe trips, on Easter Monday 8 April, were taken by the *Ravenswood* from Cardiff and the *Lady Ismay* from Bristol. On that day a westerly gale was blowing. The late Edwin Keen wrote an account of his trip in the *Lady Ismay*, accompanied by his two brothers, which was published in the Christmas 1964 issue of *Ship Ahoy*, (the quarterly magazine of the South Wales Branch of the World Ship Society). It is reproduced here with slight editions:

The season of 1911 had been a most delightful one; a summer of record temperatures, tranquil days and calm tropical weather from early May until well into October. The *Lady Ismay* had had no opportunity of showing her capabilities in bad weather, so it was not surprising that Capt. Peter and Capt. Alec should have taken the very first chance of observing her behaviour in a storm. For some days there had been strong winds from the west and north, with much rain, so that the number of passengers on this Easter Monday was not large. The *Lady Ismay* left the pontoon at Hotwells at 08.45 with Capt. Chidgey in command, and with Peter and Alec aboard. There was a strong westerly wind blowing so we knew we were in for a rough trip.

With the wind blowing straight up the Avon, white horses showed in the river at Hungroad, we started pitching off Pill and took spray aboard at the south pier, Avonmouth. I remember getting drenched before we got off Portishead and I had to go down to the engine room alleyway to dry out.

Clevedon was omitted as the landing stage was being rebuilt but we passed very close, getting whatever shelter we could under the land. We took the inside passage passing very close to the Middle Hope buoy. It was about here that the Chief Engineer, whom I remember as a small elderly man, frail looking, with light blue eyes, started nursing his engines, throttling her down as she raced.

The *Albion* backed out from Weston pier just before our arrival. Capt. Chidgey took Weston very smoothly indeed but, by then, many of our intending Ilfracombe passengers had had enough, and got off! Very few came on board and we sailed with probably not more than sixty.

Crossing Bridgewater Bay was very bad, although we were south of the Culver Sands. Even several of the ship's hands were seasick. The brother captains were stalking about on deck and below all the time and they seemed rather concerned by a small leak in the capstan engine flat.

Approaching the coast off Minehead, although slowed down, we gradually weathered on the *Ravenswood* which was outward bound from Cardiff and Penarth for Ilfracombe, and was standing across for North Hill, and making very bad weather of it. She frequently showed the whole of her port paddle wheel, then buried it completely. How often have I regretted not doing photography in those days!

Once we were under the cliffs, rock crawling, it was not too bad, but probably we had become used to the motion by then. We arrived at Ilfracombe five and three quarter hours after leaving Hotwells.

The *Lady Ismay* was advertised to run a cruise down channel from Ilfracombe, and did so, but had to put back off Bull Point. In the meantime we had a meal in the town and then walked up to Quayfields to see the steamer come alongside. The *Ravenswood* had arrived after the Lady Ismay and was one and a quarter hours late. Capt. Joe Ashford, of the Westward Ho, was in command and we afterwards heard that he was complimented on his arrival at Ilfracombe by his passengers for the way he had handled and nursed the ship on the trip down. The *Ravenswood* had to back out for the *Lady Ismay* to berth after her curtailed cruise and stood off, rolling horribly, until the latter was fast at the pier. From our seat we had a good view of the steamers surging at the pier and saw several mooring ropes part.

Soon we were back aboard for the return journey. Capt. Chidgey backed her out, but no farther than he dared, stern down channel. He was evidently afraid for his rudder, and with his eyes fixed on the big seas astern, called to the mate at the wheel, 'Is she coming around?' 'Yes'. The mate put the ship on course and handed over the wheel to one of the hands.

I was sitting in a deck chair in the lee of the funnel. The three captains were on the bridge; Peter in the starboard wing with Chidgey near him and Alec amidships. A big sea caught the ship on her port quarter and raced along her side. The helmsman somehow let her 'fall off', she rolled heavily to starboard and things started moving. Chidgey fell against Peter, knocking his breath out. Passengers, luggage, chairs and large seats were flung to leeward. Under the wing of the bridge I saw a deck chair go overboard over the top of the rail, and others vanished through the rails. I was thrown from my chair, swept across the deck, and fetched up with my shoulder against the rail. The man at the wheel lost his head for a moment when he saw her broach to. He let

Lady Ismay *arriving at Ilfracombe on Easter Monday 8 April 1912.*

Passengers aboard Lady Ismay *arriving at Ilfracombe on Easter Monday 8 April 1912.*

the wheel go and grabbed the bridge rail but Alec seized the wheel and got the ship back. Peter went below shortly after this, probably to assess the damage in the saloon. I remained on deck hoping for a repeat performance but I was disappointed – Alec saw to that! Strangely, although the confusion seemed so great at the time, I never heard of anyone being seriously injured, nor of any claim being made against the company. Later, when one of the hands came around to clip the tickets, the passenger next to me said to him, 'He ought to have got her under that one'. He replied, 'Yes. That's what Alec told him'.

By now the wind was obviously going down, but a heavy swell persisted right up to Avonmouth. The rest of the trip was uneventful, Chidgey took Weston Pier without incident and when we arrived at Hotwells I was tired – but so very happy!

An account of the *Ravenswood's* Easter Monday trip down channel appeared in the *Western Mail* on the following day:

A Lively Sea Trip from Cardiff to Ilfracombe.
Passengers Experience Worst Journey for Years.
Considering the unfavourable weather conditions, the passenger boats of P. & A. Campbell were, yesterday, wonderfully well patronised, but the trip to Ilfracombe from Cardiff was one of the worst experienced for many seasons. Messrs Campbell carried out their services as advertised with five trips being run to Weston and back, while there were about 700 passengers on the journeys to and from Bristol. Notwithstanding the heavy wind from the west, and the unfavourable outlook, about 300 trippers braved the journey to Ilfracombe on the *Ravenswood*, leaving Cardiff at about 11 o'clock. So threatening was the weather that experienced men on the docks prophesied that the *Ravenswood* would not complete the run, and that the heavy seas would compel the captain to return. A passenger commented, 'The trip was the worst I have ever known. The boat drew up at Penarth to take on a few passengers, but when off Barry I really thought that the captain would not proceed further. Practically everyone was driven below, and suffered from sea sickness, but even so, I don't think they appreciated fully the angry sea which prevailed... It rained nearly all the way down, but even if it had not it would have been impossible to keep dry on deck owing to the heavy seas and spray, which was driven from one end of the ship to the other. Such waves I have never seen, except in the Bay of Biscay; they were as high as house tops. They were topped with crests several yards high and were swept clean along the deck... When we reached Ilfracombe I had some doubt as to whether the captain would get the vessel safely alongside the pier, but this was managed all right. Personally, I never entertained any apprehension of real danger as I knew the captain so well. I had every confidence in him, and I cannot speak too highly of the skill which Capt. Ashford displayed in handling the ship. He nursed the boat with great cleverness in the way in which he manoeuvred her to meet the mountainous seas. It was, I can assure you, very uncomfortable at times but it was also the occasion for great admiration of the work of the captain...

The coal strike was settled on 6 April 1912 but it took some time before supplies were obtainable in normal quantities. It was 25 April before the *Britannia* sailed from Bristol for Govan, and did not leave there, with her new boiler, until 22 May. The *Cambria* and *Devonia* left Bristol on 8 June. The former arrived at Govan for reboilering on the following day but the *Devonia*, in tow of the tug *Alliance*, took two and a half days to reach the A.&J. Inglis yard. The *Cambria* left Govan for Cardiff on 26 June but the *Devonia* did not follow until 12 July, having had her sponsons reduced in width by 6in on either side and a new star centre fitted with her new eight-float paddle wheels. Both the *Britannia* and *Cambria* received new inner funnels, the old ones having been burned through. At the same time both steamers received new cowl tops of the deeply sloping style similar to that of the *Waverley*.

The *Ravenswood*, having been plated in with portholes during the winter, replaced the *Waverley* on the South Coast and sailed from Bristol on 15 May 1912, followed by the *Glen Rosa* on 22 May and the *Brighton Queen* on 23 May.

Alec had suggested that the *Westonia* should be renamed and submitted the name 'Clovelly' for approval by the Board of Trade. However, that name was already in use and would not be permitted. She was eventually renamed *Tintern*, the name being changed by Board of Trade minute on 5 June 1912, the day on which she entered service.

The new steamer, ordered in October 1911 for delivery at the end of April 1912, was launched at Troon on 30 May 1912, well behind schedule. Miss Nellie Campbell performed the ceremony and named the vessel *Glen Avon*. The original name chosen for her was 'Lady Margaret' but the Board of Trade would not allow it as the name was already in use.

Ravenswood arriving at Eastbourne in 1912.

Glen Rosa *arriving at Littlehampton, 1912.*

Brighton Queen *at Boulogne, 6 September 1912.*

Tintern *arriving at Penarth, 1912.*

Tintern *swinging at Tongue Head, 1912.*

Tintern *at Hotwells Landing Stage with* Westward Ho *in mid-stream, 1912.*

The Ailsa Shipbuilding Co.'s yard at Troon early in 1912. On the slipway, behind the tug, is the Glen Avon *under construction.*

Opposite: Glen Avon *about to be launched by Nellie Campbell, 30 May 1912.*

Although the *Glen Avon* was a duplicate in build of the *Lady Ismay* she presented a somewhat different appearance for a variety of reasons. The sheer of her hull was increased by 4in forward and 1.5in aft, and there were four engine room ventilators, two on either side of the reserved deckhouse, ensuring a good draught of cool air going down to the engine room. The *Glen Avon* carried a stern lifeboat which was fitted, not in swan-neck davits, but in patent Ailsa davits that ensured quick release into the water. The saloon ventilators on the after promenade deck were much smaller in diameter than those of the *Lady Ismay* but her machinery and paddle wheels were identical. The 'Bristol Channel and District Guide', the official handbook of P&A Campbell Ltd, made a curious mistake in its description of her by stating that she had 'larger boilers' than the *Lady Ismay*. In truth, her single boiler was only 6in greater in diameter. The *Lady Ismay*'s boiler had only three furnaces and it was found that when raking out the centre furnace steam pressure was apt

Glen Avon *on trials in the Firth of Clyde, 9 July 1912.*

to fall, this was rectified by giving the *Glen Avon's* boiler four furnaces. The device on her paddle boxes was a carving of the Avon Gorge at Clifton, but the most striking difference between the two ships was that the *Glen Avon's* funnel was much shorter than that of the *Lady Ismay*, which, most unusually, occurred because of a miscalculation in which the height of the fiddley casing had been deducted from the overall height of the funnel. It was also fitted with a deeply sloping cowl in contrast to the *Lady Ismay's* shallower design.

The *Glen Avon* ran her preliminary trials on 4 July 1912 and her official trials off Skelmorlie on 9 July. Her best mean speed was 16.90 knots although she made one run, with the wind and tide in her favour, of 18.05 knots. She left Troon on the evening of 9 July under the command of Capt. Daniel Ryan, master of the *Devonia* since 1905, who entered service with P&A Campbell Ltd on their purchase of the latter. Capt. J.H. Denman also returned to the Campbell fold as master of the *Barry*, and Capt. George Ayland retained command of the *Tintern*, ex-*Westonia*.

On her way south the *Glen Avon* met a heavy gale in the Irish Sea. Capt. Ryan reported that she coped superbly with the high seas but to avoid damage he thought it prudent to put into Holyhead until the gale blew itself out. She arrived in Bristol on the early morning tide of Thursday 12 July and moored at the Mardyke Wharf.

She was registered and stationed at Newport for the purpose of coping with the ever increasing traffic from the town, and from there made her maiden trip on Saturday 14 July 1912, leaving Newport at 15.00 for an afternoon cruise to

The maiden trip of the Glen Avon, *Saturday 14 July 1912. Having discharged her passengers at Hotwells Landing Stage, she is moving up to Tongue Head to swing in readiness for her return to Newport.*

Bristol under the command of Capt. James Nurcombe Webber. A full complement boarded her and the road bridge across the Usk and the river banks were lined with spectators to watch her leave. On her return up the river Usk that evening she passed the *Albion*, outward bound, which elicited much cheering from the *Glen Avon's* passengers. The *Albion* had become a great favourite with the residents of Newport but her maximum passenger capacity of 747 was beginning to prove inadequate; the *Glen Avon's* capacity of 1,066 passengers was to ease the problem.

The last sailing of the *Albion* from Newport in 1912 took place on Monday 30 July. She then left for the South Coast where she joined the *Brighton Queen, Glen Rosa* and the *Ravenswood*, the last named having replaced the *Waverley* that year. It was during this season that the *Albion* made her record passage from Brighton to Eastbourne of one hour and six minutes. This record was vouched for by Mr W.A. Pelly, Campbells' Eastbourne agent until 1939. Several faster passages have been claimed but after a detailed search of the Campbell records, the author has failed to find a single instance, and Mr Pelly was not given to making inaccurate statements.

In contrast to 1911, the summer of 1912 was exceptionally wet and very cold. In fact, during the coldest August for fifty years, frost was recorded on the Isle of Wight! September was a particularly stormy month. The late Arthur Dumbleton recalled an incident on Wednesday 5 September 1912 when he was a chocolate boy in the *Devonia*. Making her way around the Foreland, in very rough conditions, she met a tremendous freak sea about 30ft high. Young Arthur saw it coming and

Glen Avon *approaching Ilfracombe pier after lying at anchor offshore, 1912/1913.*

Glen Avon *at Newport, 1912/1913.*

Britannia *rounding the Horseshoe Bend in the river Avon, 1912.*

dived down the forward companionway. Capt. Ryan also saw it and immediately rang down 'Stop' on the engine room telegraph, nevertheless, the *Devonia* shipped it green! Ropes and deck seats were washed down the foredeck and smashed against the chartroom, causing considerable damage. The *Lady Ismay*, a short distance behind also bound for Ilfracombe, caught the same wave off Glenthorne and had a similar experience.

Apart from the weather, 1912 had been a bad season. The coal strike; the tragic loss of the White Star liner, *Titanic*, in April, which had deterred many people from taking sea trips, and the late return of the steamers from Glasgow had all conspired to reduce takings. Furthermore, P&A Campbell Ltd had, from the beginning of the season, abolished the 'Saloon' and 'Foredeck' pricing of tickets; the fares were now the same for both parts of the ships. The fares from Bristol to Ilfracombe in 1911 had been 7s 6d return, saloon, and 3s return, foredeck. In 1912 the fare was 5s.

The *Glen Rosa* returned from the South Coast on Monday 1 October but continued to run in the Bristol Channel for a short period. On returning from Bristol to Cardiff at 19.15 on Tuesday 9 October, in attempting to avoid a ship which had grounded in the Avon, she also ran aground, fortunately close to Sea Mills. A gangway was put ashore and her passengers were able to disembark without difficulty. A special train then took them from Sea Mills station to Temple Meads from where a further train took the Clevedon and Cardiff passengers home. The *Glen Rosa* later refloated, undamaged.

Westward Ho *at Bristol on a particularly high tide in 1912.*

Devonia *arriving at Penarth in 1912.*

Barry off Ilfracombe, 1912.

Passengers aboard the Barry at Ilfracombe on 30 July 1912.

Barry *arriving at Ilfracombe in 1912. P&A Campbell Ltd took a leaf out of the Red Funnel book in stationing the* Barry *at Ilfracombe from late July until the end of August. She took on coal at the Stone Bench as she had done in her Barry Railway days.*

Aboard the Lady Ismay *at Cardiff early in 1913. One of a series of photographs submitted by Capt. Alec Campbell and Mr G.E. Halstead to the Board of Trade for their approval of new deck seating.*

1913

The *Titanic* inquiry revealed that she had carried insufficient lifeboats for her passengers. There was an immediate public outcry and the Board of Trade introduced new regulations for passenger ships, not only for deep-sea vessels but also for excursion steamers, whereby extra lifeboats and life rafts were to be provided. The problem was how to provide them without sacrificing deck space – a problem which pursued excursion steamer operators for many years. During the winter of 1912/1913 Capt. Alec and Mr G.E. Halstead, of Campbells' Cardiff office, came up with a solution.

Each of the wooden, sparred deck seats in the Campbell ships contained four copper buoyancy tanks. Additional life rafts were to be fitted under the seats, these life rafts also being fitted with four copper buoyancy tanks, so that they would float off separately. They were also to be provided with grab lines, each of which, like the upper rafts, were fitted with a wooden hand grip which would cause the grab lines to float. The top seats were capable of supporting eighteen people, and with the new under rafts a total of thirty-four passengers could be supported. The Board of Trade approved the idea and Alec and Mr Halstead applied for Patent rights which were granted on 25 April 1913. Ninety of the new rafts were immediately ordered in Bristol.

The Board of Trade set a deadline of 1 November 1913 for the fitting of the extra lifeboats and life rafts. As Campbells' season usually ended in October they had until the beginning of the 1914 season to fit out all their ships, although efforts were made to have some of the steamers so fitted by Whitsun 1913. The first steamers to receive the extra lifeboats, which were carried forward of the paddle boxes, were the *Britannia, Westward Ho, Devonia, Brighton Queen, Albion, Ravenswood* and *Barry*.

Above and opposite: Devonia, *now with forward lifeboats, in Stothert's Dry Dock, Bristol, in the spring of* *1913.*

Devonia *leaving Cardiff in 1913.*

Devonia *in the river Avon, 1913/1914.*

Britannia *in the river Avon, 20 August 1913.*

Cambria *off Newquay, 1913.*

Westward Ho *off Newquay, 1913.*

Barry *leaving Bristol, 1913/1914.*

Barry *passing Pill, in the river Avon, 1913/1914.*

Lady Ismay *and* Waverley *off Penarth, 1913.*

Lady Ismay *in the river Avon, 1913.*

Capt. Alec reported to the directors, on 15 April 1913, that an offer of £10,500 had been received from Messrs. Thomas Reid & Co., Shipbrokers, of Glasgow, for the *Tintern*. The Board agreed to the sale and left the matter to Peter and Alec. At the following board meeting on 28 April Alec stated that he had accepted the offer of £10,500, (which included commission of £787 10s), from Thomas Reid & Co. who were acting on behalf of the Portuguese State Railways.

Much speculation has been made as to why the *Tintern* was sold so suddenly but the answer is revealed in the Campbell minute books. The company's bankers were anxious that the amount of their overdraft, which was fixed at £75,300, should be reduced as soon as possible. (There were mortgages on the *Lady Ismay*, *Glen Avon*, *Devonia*, *Barry* and *Tintern*). The offer for the *Tintern* came 'out of the blue' at a very opportune moment and the bank insisted that £9,700, (the amount of the offer less Reid's commission), should be paid off the overdraft immediately – a course of action which was approved by the directors and duly carried out.

The Portuguese State Railways were Caminhos de Ferro do Sul e Sueste – South & South Western Railways – who intended to use the *Tintern* as a ferry between Lisbon and Barreiro, on opposite banks of the river Tagus. P&A Campbell's secretary produced the bill of sale at the 28 April meeting which was signed and sealed. The *Tintern* sailed from Avonmouth Dock on 2 May 1913 bound for Lisbon, where she received her new and fifth name of *Alentejo*. She continued to operate on the river Tagus until being broken up in 1924.

Easter of 1913 was very early, the first Cardiff to Weston trip taking place on 19 March and the first Ilfracombe trip on the following day. The Weston sailings continued for the season but the Ilfracombe trips ceased on 27 March and did not resume until 5 May.

The *Ravenswood* was the first steamer to go south and made her first trip, from Brighton to Eastbourne and Hastings, on Thursday 20 March. A couple of days later the late paddle steamer enthusiast, Mr E.A.C. Smith, boarded her for an afternoon cruise:

I was at Brighton for the Easter weekend and on the Saturday afternoon, 22 March, went on a trip to Eastbourne aboard the Ravenswood – but we never reached there. The steamer had a good complement and the weather was good when we started – I remember that work was in progress while we sailed to fit the two extra lifeboats to conform to the new regulations following the *Titanic* disaster. On nearing Beachy Head ominous clouds gave warning of an approaching storm and on trying to round the headland to make for the pier we ran full into it. It was an alarming experience and I wondered whether we would survive it. The little ship seemed to stand on end, and rolled, pitched and jumped so much that I really feared that she might founder. Coats and hats, bags and sundry articles went overboard with most of their owners too seasick to care. Capt. Hector MacFadyen did a magnificent job of seamanship, and eventually, after struggling for about an hour, turned her around and headed for Newhaven. Landing there in various stages of discomfort the passengers were accommodated in a pub to

Ravenswood off Eastbourne, 1913/1914.

Capt. Hector McFadyen with the officers and crew of the Ravenswood, *1912/1913.*

await a special train for Brighton, where we arrived at about 11pm. Looking at the brave little ship after landing I was surprised that she had suffered no damage. That night, when the storm was at its height, shop windows along the Brighton sea front were blown in and Worthing Pier was severed, parts of it being washed away. I went to Worthing on the following day to see the pier – the seaward part looked like an island.

Glen Rosa at Hotwells Landing Stage in 1914, showing the additional lifeboat on the port quarter.

The *Brighton Queen* went south on 17 May 1913 and was followed a little later by the *Albion*, the latter being sent in preference to the *Glen Rosa* as she had a No.2 Certificate which enabled her to cross the channel. The *Albion* therefore made several trips to Boulogne as well as a number of long distance cruises to Folkestone and Ramsgate, supplementing the sailings of the *Brighton Queen* which continued to sail regularly to Boulogne and occasionally to Calais.

There was some excitement aboard the *Lady Ismay* on Tuesday 3 June 1913. While returning to Bristol after a cruise she was signalled by the Royal Line's *Royal Edward* off Clevedon. Both vessels slowed down and the *Lady Ismay* went alongside the liner to disembark five visitors who had failed to hear the 'All ashore' bell and who were thankful that they had not been taken on an involuntary trip to Canada!

At the board meeting on 22 July 1913 Capt. Alec told the directors that he and his brother had reached the conclusion that it would not be desirable to run the *Bonnie Doon* again. She was now the oldest member of the fleet, dating from 1876, and had been eclipsed by the new steamers. It was decided that she should be sold for scrap. By the end of September an offer of £700 had been accepted from Pugsley & Co., Iron Merchants, of Bathurst Wharf, Bristol, and the Bill of Sale was signed accordingly.

William Pugsley, however, had second thoughts about breaking up the *Bonnie Doon* himself and sold her on 27 October, at a profit, to a Dutch company for breaking up at Rotterdam. She left Bristol on Thursday 30 October 1913 in tow of the Dutch tug, *Gouwzee,* and passed The Lizard, eastward bound, on the following day.

The second oldest member of the fleet, the *Glen Rosa* of 1877, was also the subject of negotiation. It appears that the Bristol Docks Committee had been thinking of buying her for use as a tender for the Royal Liners to save the expense of hiring a Campbell steamer each time. At the board meeting on 29 September 1913 Alec reported that no definite decision had been made by the Docks Committee but pointed out that in the event of the proposed sale being effective it would be essential that an order should be placed with the builders of the *Glen Avon* for a new steamer, and that the order should be placed without delay to ensure delivery by Whitsun of 1914. After discussion it was agreed that the order should be placed immediately with the Ailsa Shipbuilding Co. who, it appears, had already quoted £21,275 for a duplicate of the *Glen Avon*.

1914

The Bristol Docks Committee eventually decided against the purchase of the *Glen Rosa*, but in January 1914 an agreement was made to pay P&A Campbell Ltd £1,000 per year for her hire, as and when required, with a rebate of £10 for any occasion for which she had been booked but was not used.

Before the opening of the 1914 season the remaining steamers were fitted with extra lifeboats. The *Glen Rosa* and *Waverley*, however, were required to carry only one additional boat. That of the former was carried in davits on her port quarter, and that of the *Waverley* was placed on her port side forward of the paddle box.

Capt. John West, master of the *Brighton Queen*, died suddenly on 3 April 1914. He was the son of the late Capt. Daniel West and had gained his Master's Certificate at the very early age of eighteen. He had joined the company in 1891 and took command of the *Waverley* in 1894, progressing into the *Cambria* and then the *Brighton Queen*. Capt. Hector MacFadyen was promoted to the *Brighton Queen* for the 1914 season.

The *Ravenswood* was the first steamer to enter south coast service. She left Bristol for Southampton and Brighton at 12 noon on Saturday 4 April 1914 with her flags at half-mast as a mark of respect for Capt. West's death. Her passage south was a long and stormy one. After sheltering at Ilfracombe for three days she reached Lundy, but had to shelter again until late on Friday 10 April. She reached Southampton, after a very rough passage, at 06.10 on Sunday 12 April. After coaling she left at 11.00, and reached the Palace Pier, Brighton, at 14.18 where she hurriedly took on stores in time to make her first scheduled sailing with passengers for Eastbourne at 14.50.

The new steamer was launched at Troon on Saturday 11 April 1914 by Mrs Peter Campbell and named *Glen Usk*. She was a duplicate of the *Glen Avon* but was 4.5ft longer and 1ft greater in beam. Capt. Dan Taylor had supervised her construction and she incorporated many of his ideas, including greater sheer, considerably more flare to the bows, and heavier construction than her predecessor. Her funnel was taller than the *Glen Avon*'s, (no miscalculation this time), and with its flat cowl resembled

Brighton Queen *off the South Coast, 18 August 1913.*

Waverley *in the river Avon in 1914.*

Brighton Queen *(above)*, and Albion *(below)*, leaving Bristol for the South Coast. *1914*.

A farewell blast on the Brighton Queen's *whistle as she leaves Bristol for Brighton in 1914. The* Albion *is ahead of her.*

the *Lady Ismay's*. The *Glen Usk* was fitted from the start with lifeboats forward of the paddle boxes and also carried a stern boat in quick release davits. The device on her paddle boxes has always been assumed to have been a representation of Newport Castle but it was, in fact, a carving of Raglan Castle, (situated approximately 12 miles north of Newport and a few miles from the valley of the river Usk).

The *Glen Usk* ran her trials at Skelmorlie on Wednesday 27 May 1914 and attained a mean speed of 17.16 knots. After a brief call at Kilmun she returned to Troon to bunker, leaving there at 20.30 under the command of Capt. Dan Taylor with Alec acting as mate. On her arrival at Bristol at 20.00 on the following evening they found the tide well up and the locks at both ends of the Cumberland Basin open. With Dan at the wheel and Alec at the telegraphs they took her straight through and moored at the Mardyke Wharf where a large group of spectators waited to greet her.

The three Ailsa built ships, *Lady Ismay*, *Glen Avon* and *Glen Usk*, were very well built and most beautifully finished – the Ailsa company had many years experience in the building of yachts and employed some very fine craftsmen. They were excellent sea-boats, but never became as revered as the *Britannia* and *Cambria* as they lacked the 'glamour' of speed. Nevertheless, the Ailsa ships were the 'money-spinners' of that era; their large passenger carrying capacity coupled with their low fuel bills earned the profits!

Above and below: Glen Usk *on trials in the Firth of Clyde, Wednesday 27 May 1914.*

Glen Usk *moored at the Mardyke Wharf, Bristol, on her arrival from the builders, Thursday 28 May 1914.*

The *Glen Usk* made her maiden trip, from Newport, at 09.00 on Whit Monday 1 June 1914, to Weston, Minehead and Ilfracombe. She repeated this on the following day and then went back to Bristol for a couple of days for 'touching up'. Dan Taylor commanded her during her first few weeks to see how she performed, before returning to the *Britannia*.

He was reported to have been more than satisfied with the ship in the design of which he had played such a large part. The Ailsa 'trio' followed a similar pattern to that of the famous trio of the 1890's - the *Westward Ho, Cambria* and *Britannia* – each vessel an improvement on her predecessor and each one supervised in their building by the formidable duo of Dan Taylor and Peter Campbell. The *Britannia* – 'Capt. Peter's Toy', and the *Glen Usk* – 'Capt. Taylor's Masterpiece', were, without doubt, among the finest vessels of their type.

It is interesting to note that at the time of the building of the *Glen Usk* the Ailsa Co's. Technical Manager, Mr William Steele Watson, became so infected with Capt. Peter's enthusiasm for paddle steamers that he became known as 'Paddle Watson', and that he was still remembered by that nick-name in the Ailsa yard as late as 1980, many years after his death.

The summer of 1914, although blessed with good weather, was overshadowed by the threat of impending conflict. The deteriorating political situation throughout Europe persuaded the Admiralty to hold a trial mobilisation of the fleet prior to the Royal Naval Review held in Spithead on Monday 20 July. Earlier in the season squadrons of warships had assembled off a number of coastal resorts in order to 'show the flag', and good business was enjoyed by the excursion steamers in running cruises to view the ships at close quarters and, in some cases, allowing their passengers on board.

Glen Usk *at Hotwells Landing Stage, 1914.*

Glen Usk *in the Cumberland Basin, 1914.*

At 22.30 on Tuesday 4 August 1914 King George V held a privy council at Buckingham Palace which sanctioned the proclamation of a state of war between Great Britain and Germany. The Admiralty signalled to all Royal Naval ships 'Commence hostilities against Germany'.

Strange as it may seem the declaration of war had little immediate effect on the White Funnel Fleet's South Coast services.

On Wednesday 5 August the *Albion* ran from Brighton, Eastbourne and Hastings to Folkestone but the harbour was so jammed with vessels that she was refused entry. On the same day the *Brighton Queen* went to Cowes and Southsea to witness the race between the big yachts for the Emperor's Cup; Cowes Week was in full swing.

The *Brighton Queen* was scheduled to sail to Boulogne on Thursday 6 August and was on her way from Newhaven to Brighton in readiness for her 10.00 departure when a telegram was received at the Palace Pier from the Boulogne harbourmaster stating that 'It was highly preferable that the *Brighton Queen* should not come', the harbour being too crowded. All further Boulogne trips were cancelled but the coastal trips continued; the German minelaying campaign had not yet reached the South Coast. The *Brighton Queen* sailed to Southampton on Friday 7 August, bunkered and sailed again on the following day, arriving in Bristol on Sunday 9 August to lay up.

Ravenswood *arriving at Palace Pier, Brighton, in 1914.*

Opposite above: Westward Ho *arriving at Ilfracombe on 11 June 1914.*

Opposite below: Britannia *rounding the Horseshoe Bend, river Avon, in 1914.*

Brighton Queen *arriving at Eastbourne, 1914.*

On Monday 24 August the *Ravenswood* cracked the cover of her high pressure cylinder and limped into Eastbourne Pier. The *Albion* took her in tow to off Shoreham, from where the tug *Stella* took her into the harbour; the fleet's usual base, Newhaven, being too full. The *Glen Rosa,* under the command of Capt. MacFadyen, was sent south to take over her sailings, leaving Bristol on Wednesday 26 August. After temporary repairs the *Ravenswood* left Shoreham, under her own steam, on the morning of Saturday 29 August and arrived in Bristol on the following day. At the end of their season the *Albion* docked in Bristol on Sunday 27 September and the *Glen Rosa* arrived on the 28th. Like the *Brighton Queen,* neither vessel would sail on the South Coast again.

On 7 August Alec reported to the directors that owing to a great reduction in traffic during the Bank Holiday week he had considered it advisable to lay up seven of the steamers. The exceptions were the *Lady Ismay,* which ran between Cardiff and Ilfracombe, the *Glen Usk,* running from Bristol to Weston, Clevedon, Minehead, Lynmouth and Ilfracombe, and two steamers, believed to be the *Barry* and the *Glen Avon,* running between Cardiff and Weston.

The *Barry* ended her season on Monday 14 September 1914 but put to sea again a week later. She left the south pier at Avonmouth on Monday 21 September and moored alongside the steamship *Trevilley* in Walton Bay. After embarking 368 German prisoners of war and an escort of 193 men of the Royal Scots she sailed for Dublin at 20.55. She arrived at Dublin at 10.40 on the following morning and disembarked the prisoners. On Wednesday 23 September she embarked 303 civilian prisoners, again with the escort, and left Dublin at 20.50. These were disembarked at Douglas, Isle

This photograph appeared in the Bristol Channel & District Guide *for some years after the First World War. It was reproduced in such heavily retouched form that many people thought that it had been 'faked' by superimposing one or other of the steamers. It is, however, perfectly genuine and shows the Cumberland Basin on the morning of Friday 25 September 1914 with the* Barry *(left), returning from her brief visit to Ireland and the Isle of Man to lay up. What gives the photograph a particular poignancy is the* Devonia, *moored to the basin wall, in the course of her minesweeping trials and preparation for war service.*

of Man, on her arrival at 06.00. She left Douglas at 08.30 that morning and arrived at Avonmouth at 06.00 on Friday 25 September, where the escort disembarked. The *Barry* then made her way to Bristol and docked in the Floating Harbour, rejoining her consorts, two of which were already preparing to leave their home port to play their part in what was to become known as 'The Great War'.

The down-channel trips ended on Saturday 26 September and the Cardiff to Weston sailings ended on Wednesday 30 September, the day on which the *Devonia* and *Brighton Queen* left Bristol for Devonport to begin their war service. They became the 'Pioneer' paddle minesweepers; the rest of the White Funnel Fleet was to follow.

The First World War was to change the whole aspect of British society and P&A Campbell Ltd were never again to enjoy the very profitable years. The 'Golden Era' of the White Funnel Fleet had ended.

INDEX

(Numbers in **bold** refer to illustrations)

If you are interested in purchasing other books published by Tempus,
or in case you have difficulty finding any Tempus books in your local bookshop,
you can also place orders directly through our website

www.tempus-publishing.com